W9-AZD-608

LIVING THE QUESTIONS IN Luke

A NavStudy Featuring

NAVPRESS®

BRINGING TRUTH TO LIFE

OUR GUARANTEE TO YOU

We believe so strongly in the message of our books that we are making this quality guarantee to you. If for any reason you are disappointed with the content of this book, return the title page to us with your name and address and we will refund to you the list price of the book. To help us serve you better, please briefly describe why you were disappointed. Mail your refund request to: NavPress, P.O. Box 35002, Colorado Springs, CO 80935.

The Navigators is an international Christian organization. Our mission is to reach, disciple, and equip people to know Christ and to make Him known through successive generations. We envision multitudes of diverse people in the United States and every other nation who have a passionate love for Christ, live a lifestyle of sharing Christ's love, and multiply spiritual laborers among those without Christ.

NavPress is the publishing ministry of The Navigators. NavPress publications help believers learn biblical truth and apply what they learn to their lives and ministries. Our mission is to stimulate spiritual formation among our readers.

© 2005 by The Navigators

All rights reserved. No part of this publication may be reproduced in any form without written permission from NavPress, P.O. Box 35001, Colorado Springs, CO 80935.
www.navpress.com

NAVPRESS, BRINGING TRUTH TO LIFE, and the NAVPRESS logo are registered trademarks of NavPress. Absence of ® in connection with marks of NavPress or other parties does not indicate an absence of registration of those marks.

ISBN 1-57683-861-7

Cover design by Disciple Design
Cover photo by Gary Walpole
Creative Team: Steve Parolini, Arvid Wallen, Kathy Mosier, Pat Reinheimer

Written and compiled by John Blase

Some of the anecdotal illustrations in this book are true to life and are included with the permission of the persons involved. All other illustrations are composites of real situations, and any resemblance to people living or dead is coincidental.

All Scripture quotations in this publication are taken from *THE MESSAGE* (MSG). Copyright © 1993, 1994, 1995, 1996, 2000, 2001, 2002. Used by permission of NavPress Publishing Group.

Printed in the United States of America

1 2 3 4 5 6 7 8 9 10 / 09 08 07 06 05

FOR A FREE CATALOG OF
NAVPRESS BOOKS & BIBLE STUDIES,
CALL 1-800-366-7788 (USA)
OR 1-800-839-4769 (CANADA)

CONTENTS

ABOUT THE
LIVING THE QUESTIONS
SERIES

> I want to beg you, as much as I can . . . to be patient toward all that is unsolved in your heart and try to love the questions themselves like locked rooms and like books that are written in a very foreign tongue. Do not now seek the answers, which cannot be given you because you would not be able to live them. . . . Live the questions now. Perhaps you will then gradually, without noticing it, live along some distant day into the answer.
>
> RAINER MARIA RILKE, *LETTERS TO A YOUNG POET*

Christians usually think about Jesus as the One with all the answers; the God-man with the evidence the verdict demands; a divine answer-man, sent down to earth to give us just what we need. And yes, he did give us just what we needed. Yet a careful reading of the Gospels shows that Jesus asked just as many questions as he gave outright answers. You would not have found a "The Bible says it, I believe it, and that settles it" bumper sticker on Jesus' backpack. It was more like, "This is God's Word. Stop and think about it, and let's talk about it."

However, the perception of Jesus as the divine answer-man appeals to a great many people. Life has questions, so you go to the Scriptures, look on the right page, find the answers, and everything's good. But while that works great for algebra class, it just doesn't seem to work well for this thing called *life*. Could the "divine answer-man" approach be too simplistic? Too one-dimensional for such a deep character as Jesus Christ? For one, it seems to leave you and me, the children of

God, out of the picture. We're not colaborers with God; we're just laborers.

Jesus went about doing good. Apparently part of this "good" was asking great questions—questions that would cause people to stop and pause and ponder the things they were living for and what might be worth dying for; questions not bound by a calendar but applicable to the ages; questions as poignant today as they were then.

The book you hold in your hand takes the approach of looking at the questions found in the Gospels—the questions Jesus asked. The questions are specific to the text of Eugene Peterson's *The Message*. I'm talking about questions such as, "All this time and money wasted on fashion—do you think it makes that much difference?" or "Who needs a doctor: the healthy or the sick?" Our temptation might be to respond quickly because we think we know the answers. But what if these questions must be lived? Lived out in dimensions such as friendship, family, and church? Lived out in locales such as homes, classrooms, and forests primeval? Lived by the flesh and blood whose main focus is the future, and lived by those who think mainly of the past? And what if living out these questions might lead us one day, gradually, without noticing it, into The Answer—the One who described himself as the way, truth, and life?

Live the questions now.

HOW TO USE THIS DISCUSSION GUIDE

1. This NavStudy is meant to be completed on your own *and* in a small group. You'll want to line up your study group ahead of time. A group of four to six is optimal—any bigger and one or more members will likely be shut out of discussions. Your small group can also be two. Each person will need his or her own copy of this book.

2. Lessons open with a Scripture passage intended to help you to prepare your heart and mind for the content that follows. Don't skip over this preparation time. Use it to reflect, slow down from a busy life, and transition into your study time.

3. *Read* the Scripture passages and other readings in each lesson. Let it all soak in. Re-read if necessary. There's no blue ribbon for finishing quickly. Make notes in the white space on the page. If you like journaling, think of this as a space to journal. If you don't like journaling, just think of it as space to "think out loud on paper."

4. *Think* about what you read. Respond to the questions we've provided. Always ask, "What does this mean?" and "Why does this matter?" about the readings. Compare different Bible translations for Scripture readings. Respond to the questions we've provided, and then discuss the questions when you're in your small group. Allow the experience of others to broaden your wisdom. You'll be stretched—called upon to evaluate what you've discovered and asked to make practical sense of it. In community, that stretching can often be painful and sometimes even embarrassing. But your willingness to be transparent—your openness to the possibility of personal growth—will reap great rewards.

5. *Pray* as you go through the entire session: before you read a word, in the middle of your thinking process, when you get stuck on a concept or passage, and as you approach the time when you'll explore

these passages and thoughts together in a small group. Pause when you need to ask God for inspiration or when you need to cry out in frustration. Compose a prayer prompted by what you've uncovered in the readings and your responses to the "Think" questions.

6. *Live.* (That's "live" as in "rhymes with give" as in "Give me something I can really use in my life.") This is a place to choose one thing you can do to live out the question posed in the lesson. Don't try to craft a plan that is lofty or unreachable. Choose something small, something doable. Then, in your small group, talk about this "one thing." Commit to following through on your idea, wrestle with what that means in practical terms, and call upon your group members to hold you accountable.

7. *Follow up.* Don't let the life application drift away without action. Be accountable to small-group members and refer to previous "Live" as in "rhymes with give" sections often. Take time at the beginning of each new study to review. See how you're doing.

After going through each week's study on your own, it's time to sit down with others and go deeper. Here are a few thoughts on how to make the most of your small-group discussion time.

Set ground rules. You don't need many. Here are two:

First, you'll want group members to make a commitment to the entire ten-week study. Significant personal growth happens when group members spend enough time together to really get to know each other. Hit-and-miss attendance can hinder this growth.

Second, agree together that everyone's story is important. Time is a valuable commodity, so if you have an hour to spend together, do your best to give each person ample time to express concerns, pass along insights, and generally feel like a participating member of the group. Small-group discussions are not monologues. However, a one-person-dominated discussion isn't always a bad thing. Not only is your role in a small group to explore and expand your own understanding, it's also to support one another. If someone truly needs more of the floor, give it to him or her. There will be times when the needs of the one outweigh the needs of the many. Use good judgment and allow extra space when needed. *Your* time might be next week.

Meet regularly. Choose a time and place, and stick to it. Consistency removes stress that could otherwise frustrate discussion and subsequent personal growth.

Follow the book outline. Each week, open your small-group time with prayer, and read aloud the reflective Scripture passage that opens the lesson. Then go through the study together, reading each section aloud and discussing it with your group members. Tell others what you wrote. Write down new insights gleaned from other group members. Wrestle the questions together. When you get to the "Pray" section, ask for volunteers willing to read aloud their written prayers. Finally, spend a few minutes talking together about each person's "one thing" and how to achieve that goal.

Talk openly. If you enter this study with shields up, you're probably not alone. And you're not a "bad person" for your hesitation to unpack your life in front of friends or strangers. Maybe you're skeptical about the value of revealing to others the deepest parts of who you are. Maybe you're simply too afraid of what might fall out of the suitcase. You don't have to go to a place where you're uncomfortable. If you want to sit and listen, offer a few thoughts, or even express a surface level of your own pain, go ahead. But don't neglect what brings you to this place—that longing for meaning. You can't ignore it away. Dip your feet in the water of brutally honest discussion, and you may choose to dive in. There is healing here.

Stay on task. Refrain from sharing material that falls into the "too much information" category. Don't spill unnecessary stuff. If structure isn't your group's strength, try a few minutes of general comments about the study, and then take each question one at a time and give everyone in the group a chance to respond.

"If you only love the lovable, do you expect
a pat on the back?" (Luke 6:32)

Before You Begin

Take some time to reflect and prepare your heart and mind
for this study. Read the following Scripture passage. Soak
up God's Word. There's no hurry. Then, when you're ready,
turn the page and begin.

MALACHI 1:7-10

"When you say, 'The altar of GOD is not important anymore;
worship of GOD is no longer a priority,' that's defiling. And
when you offer worthless animals for sacrifices in worship,
animals that you're trying to get rid of—blind and sick and
crippled animals—isn't that defiling? Try a trick like that
with your banker or your senator—how far do you think it
will get you?" GOD-of-the-Angel-Armies asks you.

"Get on your knees and pray that I will be gracious to
you. You priests have gotten everyone in trouble. With this
kind of conduct, do you think I'll pay attention to you?" GOD-
of-the-Angel-Armies asks you.

"Why doesn't one of you just shut the Temple doors and
lock them? Then none of you can get in and play at religion
with this silly, empty-headed worship. I am not pleased. The
GOD-of-the-Angel-Armies is not pleased. And I don't want
any more of this so-called worship!"

READ

Luke 6:24-38

> But it's trouble ahead if you think you have it made.
> What you have is all you'll ever get.
>
> And it's trouble ahead if you're satisfied with yourself.
> Your *self* will not satisfy you for long.
>
> And it's trouble ahead if you think life's all fun and
>   games.
> There's suffering to be met, and you're going to meet it.

"There's trouble ahead when you live only for the approval of others, saying what flatters them, doing what indulges them. Popularity contests are not truth contests—look how many scoundrel preachers were approved by your ancestors! Your task is to be true, not popular.

"To you who are ready for the truth, I say this: Love your enemies. Let them bring out the best in you, not the worst. When someone gives you a hard time, respond with the energies of prayer for that person. If someone slaps you in the face, stand there and take it. If someone grabs your shirt, giftwrap your best coat and make a present of it. If someone takes unfair advantage of you, use the occasion to practice the servant life. No more tit-for-tat stuff. Live generously.

"Here is a simple rule of thumb for behavior: Ask yourself what you want people to do for you; then grab the initiative and do it for *them*! **If you only love the lovable, do you expect a pat on the back?** Run-of-the-mill sinners do that. If you only help those who help you, do you expect a medal? Garden-variety sinners do that. If you only give for what you hope to get out of it, do you think that's charity? The stingiest of pawnbrokers does that.

"I tell you, love your enemies. Help and give without expecting a return. You'll never—I promise—regret it. Live out this God-created identity the way our Father lives toward us, generously and graciously, even when we're at our worst, Our Father is kind; you be kind.

"Don't pick on people, jump on their failures, criticize their faults—unless, of course, you want the same treatment. Don't condemn those who are down; that hardness can boomerang. Be easy on people; you'll find life a lot easier. Give away your life; you'll find life given back, but not merely given back—given back with bonus and blessing. Giving, not getting, is the way. Generosity begets generosity."

THINK   "If you only love the lovable, do you expect a pat on the back?"

- What is your immediate response to this question?
- Why do you think you responded in this way?
- What do you think of Jesus' "simple rule of thumb for behavior"? Does it in any way describe your behavior? If so, how?
- Think about this reworking of Jesus' words: "Give a pat on the back to the unlovable, pin a medal on those who cannot help you in any way, and give to charity and never write it off your income tax." Do you find it foolish? Why or why not?
- "Don't pick on people, jump on their failures, criticize their faults. . . . Be easy on people." Do you think Jesus is being just a little soft here? Why or why not? How does this compare with the way you relate to others?

READ

From *In the Presence of Fear*, by Wendell Berry[1]

XVIII. In a time such as this, when we have been seriously and most cruelly hurt by those who hate us, and when we must consider ourselves to be gravely threatened by those same people, it is hard to speak of the ways of peace and to remember that Christ enjoined us to love our enemies, but this is no less necessary for being difficult.

XIX. Even now we dare not forget that since that attack of Pearl Harbor—to which the present attack has been often and not usefully compared—we humans have suffered an almost uninterrupted sequence of wars, none of which has brought peace or made us more peaceable.

XXI. What leads to peace is not violence, but peaceableness, which is not passivity, but an alert, informed, practiced, and active state of being. We should recognize that while we have extravagantly subsidized the means of war, we have almost totally neglected the ways of peaceableness. We have, for example, several national military academies, but not one peace academy. We have ignored the teachings and examples of Christ, Gandhi, Martin Luther King, and other peaceable leaders. And here we have an inescapable duty to notice also that war is profitable, whereas the means of peaceableness, being cheap or free, make no money.

XXVI. The complexity of our present trouble suggests as never before that we need to change our present concept of education. Education is not properly an industry, and its proper use is not to serve industries, neither by job-training nor by industrial-subsidized research. Its proper use is to enable citizens to live lives that are economically, politically, socially, and culturally responsible. This cannot be done by gathering or "accessing" what we now call "information"—which is to say facts without context and therefore without priority. A proper education enables young people to put their lives in order, which means knowing what things are more important than other things; it means putting first things first.

XXVII. The first thing we must begin to teach our children (and learn ourselves) is that we cannot spend and consume endlessly. We have got to learn to save and conserve. We do need a "new economy," but one that is founded on thrift and care, on saving and conserving, not on excess and waste. An economy based on waste is inherently and hopelessly violent, and war is its inevitable by-product. We need a peaceable economy.

THINK "If you only love the lovable, do you expect a pat on the back?"

- Berry's words were written after September 11, 2001. What are your first reactions to them?
- How hard is it for you to imagine that the questions Jesus asked have anything to do with an economy? Think about these two statements, the first from Jesus: "Giving, not getting, is the way. Generosity begets generosity." And the second from Berry: "The first thing we must begin to teach our children (and learn ourselves) is that we cannot spend and consume endlessly. We have got to learn to save and conserve."
- What other similarities do you see between Jesus' and Berry's words?
- Do you think we're training our children to be even remotely like what Christ has called us to be? Why or why not?

READ

From *Resistance*, by Barry Lopez[2]

After university I and my friends had scattered abroad—to Brussels, Caracas, Sapporo, Melbourne, Jakarta, any promising corner. Two or three went deep upriver on the Orinoco or out onto the plateaus of Tibet and Ethiopia. We had come to regard the work of writers and artists in our country as too compliant, as failing to expose or indict the escalating nerve of corporate institutions, the increasing connivance of government with business, or the cowardice of those reporting the news. In the 1970s and '80s, we thought of our artists and writers as people gardening their reputations, while the families of our neighborhoods disintegrated into depression and anger, the schools flew apart, and species winked out. It was the triumph of adolescence, in a nation that wanted no part of its elders' remonstrance or any conversion to their doubt.

The years passed. We had no plan. We had no hope. We had no religion. We had faith. It was our belief that within the histories of other, older cultures we would find cause not to be incapacitated by the ludicracy of our own. It was our intuition that even in those cultures into which our own had injected its peculiar folklore—that success is financial achievement, that the future is better, that life is an entertainment—we would encounter enduring stories to trade in. We thought we might be able to discern a path in stories and performances rooted in disparaged pasts that would spring our culture out of its adolescence. . . .

Our goal is simple: we want our country to flourish. Our dilemma is simple: we cannot tell our people a story that sticks. It is not that no one believes what we say, that no one knows, that none of our countrymen cares. It is not that their outspoken objections have been silenced by the rise at home of local cadres of enforcement and shadow operatives. It is not that they do not understand. It is that they cannot act. And the response to tyranny of every sort, if it is to work, must always be this: dismantle it. Take it apart. Scatter its defenders and its proponents, like a flock of starlings fed to a hurricane.

Our strategy is this: we believe if we can say what many already know in such a way as to incite courage, if the image or the word or the act breaches the indifference by which people survive, day to day, enough will protest that by their physical voices alone they will stir the hurricane.

THINK   *"If you only love the lovable, do you expect a pat on the back?"*

- Lopez's work is fiction. How do you feel about what you read?
- The title of Lopez's book is *Resistance*. And that is what Jesus is talking about in the passage from Luke 6 — resisting the pull of society, culture, whatever you want to call it, and living for a higher cause. Write down what Lopez's words provoke in you, keeping in mind what Jesus said about enemies, generosity, and so on.
- What is your response to the "tyranny" of our selfishness?
- Can we "incite courage" in ourselves and others, so as to "stir the hurricane" of righteousness? How would we go about that?

READ

From *The Clown in the Belfry*, by Frederick Buechner[3]

When Henry James, of all people, was saying goodbye once to his young nephew Billy, his brother William's son, he said something that the boy never forgot. And of all the labyrinthine and impenetrably subtle things that that most labyrinthine and impenetrable old romancer could have said, what he did say was this: "There are three things that are important in human life. The first is to be kind. The second is to be kind. The third is to be kind."

Be kind because although kindness is not by a long shot that same thing as holiness, kindness is one of the doors that holiness enters the world through, enters us through — not just gently kind but sometimes fiercely kind.

Be kind enough to yourselves not just to play it safe with your lives for your own sakes but to spend at least part of your lives like drunken sailors — for God's sake, if you believe in God, for the world's sake, if you believe in the world — and thus to come alive truly.

Be kind enough to others to listen, beneath all the words they speak, for that usually unspoken hunger for holiness which I believe is part of even the unlikeliest of us because by listening to it and cherishing it maybe we can help bring it to birth both in them and in ourselves.

Be kind to this nation of ours by remembering that New Haven, New Hope, Shalom, are the names not just of our oldest towns but of our holiest dreams which most of the time are threatened by the madness of no enemy without as dangerously as they are threatened by our own madness within.

"You have tasted of the kindness of the Lord," Peter wrote in his letter, and ultimately that, of course, is the kindness, the holiness, the sainthood and sanity, we are all of us called to. So that by God's grace we may "grow up to salvation" at last.

THINK   "If you only love the lovable, do you expect a pat
             on the back?"

- Do you agree with Henry James' advice to his nephew? Why or why not?
- Don't miss Buechner's note that there are two ways of being kind: "gently kind" and "fiercely kind." How would you define the difference between them?
- How do you feel about this sentence: "Be kind enough to yourselves not just to play it safe with your lives for your own sakes but to spend at least part of your lives like drunken sailors"?
- Consider this quote for a moment: "Our holiest dreams which most of the time are threatened by the madness of no enemy without as dangerously as they are threatened by our own madness within." What is God saying to you through this thought?

PRAY

Look back at the "Think" sections. Ruminate on your responses. Let them distill into a prayer, and then write that prayer below.

Our Father, who is kind . . .

The issue of prayer is not prayer; the issue of prayer is God.

ABRAHAM HESCHEL

LIVE

"If you only love the lovable, do you expect a pat on the back?"

The challenge now is to take this question further along—to live out this question. Think of one thing, *just one*, that you can personally do to wrestle with the question, inhabit the character of it, and live it in everyday life. In the following space, jot down your thoughts on this "one thing." Read the Scripture and quotes that follow for additional inspiration. During the coming week, pray about this "one thing," talk with a close friend about it, and learn to live the question.

One thing . . .

We are at our best when we live for others.

Edward Abbey

"Be easy on people; you'll find life a lot easier."

Luke 6:37

Live the questions now. Perhaps you will then gradually, without noticing it, live along some distant day into the answer.
RAINER MARIA RILKE, *LETTERS TO A YOUNG POET*

LESSON 2

"Is this what you were expecting?" (Luke 7:23)

Before You Begin

Take some time to reflect and prepare your heart and mind for this study. Read the following Scripture passage. Soak up God's Word. There's no hurry. Then, when you're ready, turn the page and begin.

Isaiah 61:1-3

The Spirit of God, the Master, is on me
    because God anointed me.
He sent me to preach good news to the poor,
    heal the heartbroken,
Announce freedom to all captives,
    pardon all prisoners.
God sent me to announce the year of his grace—
    a celebration of God's destruction of our enemies—
    and to comfort all who mourn,
To care for the needs of all who mourn in Zion,
    give them bouquets of roses instead of ashes,
Messages of joy instead of news of doom,
    a praising heart instead of a languid spirit.

READ

Luke 7:18-30

John's disciples reported back to him the news of all these events taking place. He sent two of them to the Master to ask the question, "Are you the One we've been expecting, or are we still waiting?"

The men showed up before Jesus and said, "John the Baptizer sent us to ask you, 'Are you the One we've been expecting, or are we still waiting?'"

In the next two or three hours Jesus healed many from diseases, distress, and evil spirits. To many of the blind he gave the gift of sight. Then he gave his answer: "Go back and tell John what you have just seen and heard:

The blind see,
The lame walk,
Lepers are cleansed,
The deaf hear,
The dead are raised,
The wretched of the earth
     have God's salvation hospitality extended to them.

"**Is this what you were expecting?** Then count yourselves fortunate!"

After John's messengers left to make their report, Jesus said more about John to the crowd of people. "What did you expect when you went out to see him in the wild? A weekend camper? Hardly. What then? A sheik in silk pajamas? Not in the wilderness, not by a long shot. What then? A messenger from God? That's right, a messenger! Probably the greatest messenger you'll ever hear. He is the messenger Malachi announced when he wrote,

I'm sending my messenger on ahead
To make the road smooth for you.

"Let me lay it out for you as plainly as I can: No one in history surpasses John the Baptizer, but in the kingdom he prepared you for, the lowliest person is ahead of him. The ordinary and disreputable people who heard John, by being baptized by him into the kingdom, are the clearest evidence; the Pharisees and religious officials would have nothing to do with such a baptism, wouldn't think of giving up their place in line to their inferiors."

THINK   "Is this what you were expecting?"

- What is your immediate response to this question?
- Why do you think you responded in this way?
- Do you think this is what John's disciples were expecting? Why or why not?
- Go back through the passage and underline each time the word *expect* or *expecting* is used.
- Think about the expectations you bring to your relationship with Jesus—we all have them. Try to list a few.
- So far, has Jesus been what you were expecting?

READ

From *A New Kind of Christian*, by Brian D. McLaren[1]

"What does a pastor do when he's having questions and doubts of his own? Can he stand up in his pulpit and say, 'Brothers and sisters, for the past three months, God hasn't seemed real to me. I have faith that God will seem real to me again in the future, but to be honest, God doesn't seem real to me today'? What does a pastor do when he questions the stock answers he's supposed to be convincing others of?"

Neo pressed his lips together, squinted his eyes, and nodded his head, as if to say, "Go on."

And then it all flowed out: "Remember when I told you . . . that I felt like a fundamentalist? Well, I feel like a fundamentalist who's losing his grip — whose fundamentals are cracking and fraying and falling apart and slipping through my fingers. It's like I thought I was building my house on rock, but it turned out to be ice, and now global warming has hit, and the ice is melting and everything is crumbling. That's scary, you know? I went to seminary right out of college, and it was great, and I thought I was getting the truth, you know, the whole truth and nothing but the truth. Now I've been a pastor for fourteen years, and for this last year or so I feel like I'm running out of gas. It's not just burnout. It's more like I'm losing my faith — well, not exactly that, but I feel that I'm losing the whole framework for my faith. You know, I keep pushing everything into these little cubbyholes, these little boxes, the little systems I got in seminary and even before that — in Sunday school and summer camp and from my parents. But life is too messy to fit. And I'm supposed to be preaching the truth, but I'm not even sure what the truth is anymore, and — that's it, really — I just feel dishonest whenever I try to preach. I used to love to preach, but now every time . . . when I start to prepare a sermon, it's agonizing and . . . and people come to me with their problems and I used to be so sure of what to say but now I try to act confident but I don't know. The only thing I'm confident about is that I don't have all the answers any-more. I'm sorry. I'm not making any sense."

"No, you're making more sense than you realize," he said, and then he started working on me. . . .

"Daniel, I think you're suffering from an immigration prob-lem, something I have a bit of experience with, you know? You have a modern faith, a faith you developed in your homeland of modernity. But you're immigrating to a new land, a postmodern world. You feel like you don't fit in either world. You can't decide whether to settle in a little ghetto or to move out into the new land. But you can't make the transition to the other side alone. You need a sponsor—someone who has already settled and acclimated, who can help you do the same."

THINK   "Is this what you were expecting?"

- What is your initial reaction to this passage?
- Have you ever had any feelings like the ones Daniel expressed? Try not to get sidetracked on the words *modern* and *post-modern*.
- If so, write them out.
- And if so, is this what you were expecting from your faith journey—a kind of vagueness instead of a certainty you'd prefer?
- What do you think is going on?
- Are you handling this on your own, or do you have a sponsor?

READ

From *Your God Is Too Safe*, by Mark Buchanan[2]

I did a funeral once for a lady who was a Christian, but few of her many children and grandchildren were. I thought I spoke the gospel clearly and boldly. Afterward, a woman came up to me. "Thank you," she said. "That was so *nice* what you said. It was really *nice*. I'm religious, too. The family always asks me to pray for the weather when we go golfing."

I reckon this: the idol of the nice god, the safe god, has done more damage to biblical faith—more damage to people coming to faith—than the caricature of the tyrant god ever did. The despotic god, howling his rage, wielding punishment with both ransacking destruction and surgical precision, at least inspired something in us. We were afraid. We wanted to appease. But this Milquetoast-Pampering deity is nothing but a cosmic lackey, an errand boy we call on to make our golf games pleasant or to help us escape reality for a little while and then summarily dismiss. Worship him? Revere him? Die for him? Believe that he died a cruel and bloody death for us? You must be kidding.

It is a strange habit of ours, that we fling so widely to the extremes but rarely find the middle. God's wrath and sovereignty we easily caricature into tyranny. And God's kindness and tender mercies we just as easily transmute into mere niceness. Meanwhile, the God who actually is—the God whose ways of speaking and acting and being are disclosed to us in Scripture—continues through Christ, "full of grace and truth," to come along "that which is his own." And, as before, "his own do not receive him" because they "do not recognize him" (John 1:10,11,14). Scripture elsewhere tells us that the "ruler of the air has blinded our eyes" to the truth. But one of the main ways the devil has done that is through the cult of the safe god. The safe god has pretty much killed the power of imagination in us, and so when the real God comes into our midst, we mostly don't even bother to look up.

THINK   "Is this what you were expecting?"

- Do you think Buchanan is on to something here? Why or why not?
- Do you see any parallels between the words of Buchanan and McLaren? If so, what?
- Think about this: Could it be that some of the angst associated with a modern view of God is really angst over a safe and manageable God? That the answer is not necessarily a postmodern view of God but a more biblical view of him?
- Don't miss this statement: "The safe god has pretty much killed the power of imagination in us, and so when the real God comes into our midst, we mostly don't even bother to look up." Look at what the real God did when he showed up in Luke 7. Does that sound anything like the kind of God you're *expecting* to show up in your life? If not, what are you expecting?

READ

From *The Lion, the Witch and the Wardrobe*, by C. S. Lewis[3]

> "Is — is he a man?" asked Lucy.
>
> "Aslan a man!" said Mr. Beaver sternly. "Certainly not. I tell you he is the King of the wood and the son of the great Emperor-Beyond-the-Sea. Don't you know who is the King of Beasts? Aslan is a lion — *the* Lion, the great Lion."
>
> "Ooh!" said Susan, "I thought he was a man. Is he — quite safe? I shall feel rather nervous about meeting a lion."
>
> "That you will, dearie, and no mistake," said Mrs. Beaver, "if there's anyone who can appear before Aslan without their knees knocking, they're either braver than most or else just silly."
>
> "Then he isn't safe?" said Lucy.
>
> "Safe?" said Mr. Beaver. "Don't you hear what Mrs. Beaver tells you? Who said anything about safe? 'Course he isn't safe. But he's good. He's the King, I tell you."

THINK   "Is this what you were expecting?"

- Do the readings and questions in this lesson make you "feel rather nervous"? Why or why not?
- Take some time to try to flesh out the differences between a safe God and a good God. If you need to, make two columns, one with the heading "safe" and one with the heading "good." Then just write.
- What does everyday spirituality look like for someone serving a safe God? A good God?

PRAY

Look back at the "Think" sections. Ruminate on your responses. Let them distill into a prayer, and then write that prayer below.

Dangerous Wonder . . .

The issue of prayer is not prayer; the issue of prayer is God.

ABRAHAM HESCHEL

LIVE   "Is this what you were expecting?"

The challenge now is to take this question further along—to live out this question. Think of one thing, *just one*, that you can personally do to wrestle with the question, inhabit the character of it, and live it in everyday life. In the following space, jot down your thoughts on this "one thing." Read the quotes that follow for additional inspiration. During the coming week, pray about this "one thing," talk with a close friend about it, and learn to live the question.

One thing . . .

I don't believe in God.

                                        Harvard student

Sit down and tell me what kind of God you don't believe in. I probably don't believe in that God either.

                                        George Buttrick

Principles are what people have instead of God.

                                        Frederick Buechner

Live the questions now. Perhaps you will then gradually, without noticing it, live along some distant day into the answer.
RAINER MARIA RILKE, *LETTERS TO A YOUNG POET*

"Which of the two would be more grateful?" (Luke 7:42)

Before You Begin

Take some time to reflect and prepare your heart and mind for this study. Read the following Scripture passage. Soak up God's Word. There's no hurry. Then, when you're ready, turn the page and begin.

PSALM 118:1-4

Thank GOD because he's good,
    because his love never quits.
Tell the world, Israel,
    "His love never quits."
And you, clan of Aaron, tell the world,
    "His love never quits."
And you who fear GOD, join in,
    "His love never quits."

READ

Luke 7:36-47

One of the Pharisees asked him over for a meal. He went to the Pharisee's house and sat down at the dinner table. Just then a woman of the village, the town harlot, having learned that Jesus was a guest in the home of the Pharisee, came with a bottle of very expensive perfume and stood at his feet, weeping, raining tears on his feet. Letting down her hair, she dried his feet, kissed them, and anointed them with the perfume. When the Pharisee who had invited him saw this, he said to himself, "If this man was the prophet I thought he was, he would have known what kind of woman this is who is falling all over him."

Jesus said to him, "Simon, I have something to tell you."

"Oh? Tell me."

"Two men were in debt to a banker. One owed five hundred silver pieces, the other fifty. Neither of them could pay up, and so the banker canceled both debts. **Which of the two would be more grateful?**"

Simon answered, "I suppose the one who was forgiven the most."

"That's right," said Jesus. Then turning to the woman, but speaking to Simon, he said, "Do you see this woman? I came to your home; you provided no water for my feet, but she rained tears on my feet and dried them with her hair. You gave me no greeting, but from the time I arrived she hasn't quit kissing my feet. You provided nothing for freshening up, but she has soothed my feet with perfume. Impressive, isn't it? She was forgiven many, many sins, and so she is very, very grateful. If the forgiveness is minimal, the gratitude is minimal."

THINK   "Which of the two would be more grateful?"

- What is your immediate response to this question?
- Why do you think you responded in this way?

- Take a moment to go back through the passage and picture it in your mind. What are some words you would use to describe the scene?
- If you had to choose just one word, what would it be?
- What is your reaction to Jesus' behavior in this passage?
- What do you think about this statement: "If the forgiveness is minimal, the gratitude is minimal"?

READ

From *Messy Spirituality*, by Mike Yaconelli[1]

Christianity is not for people who think religion is a pleasant distraction, a nice alternative, or a positive influence. Messy spirituality is a good term for the place where desperation meets Jesus. More often than not, in Jesus' day, desperate people who tried to get to Jesus were surrounded by religious people who either ignored or rejected those who were seeking to have their hunger for God filled. Sadly, not much has changed over the years.

Desperate people don't do well in churches. They don't fit, and they don't cooperate in the furthering of their starvation. "Church people" often label "desperate people" as strange and unbalanced. But when desperate people get a taste of God, they can't stay away from him, no matter what everyone around them thinks.

Desperate is a strong word. That's why I like it. People who are desperate are rude, frantic, and reckless. Desperate people are explosive, focused, and uncompromising in their desire to get what they want. Someone who is desperate will crash through the veil of niceness. The New Testament is filled with desperate people, people who barged into private dinners, screamed at Jesus until they had his attention, or destroyed the roof of someone's house to get to him. People who are desperate for spirituality very seldom worry about the mess they make on their way to be with Jesus.

THINK   "Which of the two would be more grateful?"

- Yaconelli's first paragraph ends with, "Sadly, not much has changed over the years." Do you agree or disagree? Why?
- Who comes to mind when you think of someone who is desperate for Jesus?
- What about this person makes that word applicable?

- Do you admire him? Tolerate her? Avoid him?
- What about you? Would those around you describe you as desperate?

READ

From *Between Noon and Three*, by Robert Farrar Capon[2]

Whenever someone attempts to introduce a radically different insight to people whose minds have been formed by an old and well-worked-out way of thinking, he or she is up against an obstacle. As Jesus said, their taste for the old wine is so well established that they invariably prefer it to the new. More than that, the new wine, still fermenting, seems to them so obviously and dangerously full of power that they will not even consider putting it into their old and fragile wineskins.

But now try to see the point of the biblical imagery of winemaking a little more abstractly. The new insight is always at odds with the old way of looking at things. Even if the teacher's audience were to try earnestly to take it in, the only intellectual devices they would have to pick it up with are the categories of the old system with which it conflicts. Hence the teacher's problem: if he leaves in his teaching a single significant scrap of the old system, they, by their very effort to understand, will go to that scrap rather than to the point he is making and, having done that, will understand the new only insofar as it can be made to agree with the old—which is, not at all.

Perhaps the phrase "precluding the conversion of species in an argument" will do for a name for this teaching technique that Jesus uses in healing on the Sabbath, and that I have used in presenting you with grace in the context of an adultery. Were Jesus to have waited till sundown to heal the man's hand, the Pharisees would have seen his good deed as congruent with everything else they already knew. If they had then tried to put a messianic interpretation on it, they would have envisioned Jesus as the kind of Messiah they were ready for (a victorious and immortal one) and not as the kind he knew himself to be (a suffering and dying one). He was at pains, you see, to present them with a proposition that was totally unacceptable to them. . . .

Note too, please, that this precluding of the conversion of

the species is not an incidental device in Jesus' hands; it is his chief method. He comes from Galilee, whence arises no Messiah. His disciples are a ragtag lot of outcasts, likewise from Galilee. He consorts with a Samaritan woman, he eats with publicans and sinners, he is a glutton and a winebibber, he dies accursed, hung on a tree—and so on and on. . . . Accordingly, he gives them not one scrap to confirm their present view—or, more accurately, he always includes one solidly unacceptable scrap on which their minds will gag.

THINK "Which of the two would be more grateful?"

- How do you react to this passage? Write down any significant words or phrases.
- Think about Capon's words in light of this passage from Luke. What were some of the "scraps" the Pharisee gagged on?
- What "new wine" do you think Jesus was inviting the Pharisee to drink?

READ

From *The Wild Man's Journey*, by Richard Rohr and Joseph Martos[3]

There are two ways of being a prophet. One is to tell the enslaved they can be free. It is the difficult path of Moses. The second is to tell those who think they are free that they are in fact enslaved. This is the even more difficult path of Jesus.

THINK   "Which of the two would be more grateful?"

- This is a short reading; in fact, it's just a quote. However, there is much here, so go slowly. Take Rohr's statement and apply it to the Scripture passage. Why would the Pharisee believe he was free when he was "in fact enslaved"?
- If we let Jesus be Jesus (always a good choice), that leaves essentially two other characters in the room: Simon and the woman. Which one most closely resembles you? Why? If you answered Simon, what scraps are you gagging on?

PRAY

Look back at the "Think" sections. Ruminate on your responses.
Let them distill into a prayer, and then write that prayer below.

I'm desperate for You . . .

The issue of prayer is not prayer; the issue of prayer is God.

ABRAHAM HESCHEL

LIVE   "Which of the two would be more grateful?"

The challenge now is to take this question further along—to live out
this question. Think of one thing, *just one*, that you can personally
do to wrestle with the question, inhabit the character of it, and live
it in everyday life. In the following space, jot down your thoughts on
this "one thing." Read the quotes that follow for additional inspiration. During the coming week, pray about this "one thing," talk with a
close friend about it, and learn to live the question.

One thing...

They were good in the worst sense of the word.

Mark Twain

He got all "A's" and flunked life.

Walker Percy

> Live the questions now. Perhaps you will then gradually, without
> noticing it, live along some distant day into the answer.
> RAINER MARIA RILKE, *LETTERS TO A YOUNG POET*

"Which of the three became a neighbor to
the man attacked by robbers?" (Luke 10:36)

Before You Begin

Take some time to reflect and prepare your heart and mind
for this study. Read the following Scripture passage. Soak
up God's Word. There's no hurry. Then, when you're ready,
turn the page and begin.

PSALM 139:13-16

> Oh yes, you shaped me first inside, then out;
>> you formed me in my mother's womb.
> I thank you, High God—you're breathtaking!
>> Body and soul, I am marvelously made!
>> I worship in adoration—what a creation!
> You know me inside and out,
>> you know every bone in my body;
> You know exactly how I was made, bit by bit,
>> how I was sculpted from nothing into something.
> Like an open book, you watched me grow from
>>> conception to birth;
>> all the stages of my life were spread out before you,
> The days of my life all prepared
>> before I'd even lived one day.

READ

Luke 10:25-37

Just then a religion scholar stood up with a question to test Jesus. "Teacher, what do I need to do to get eternal life?"

He answered, "What's written in God's Law? How do you interpret it?"

He said, "That you love the Lord your God with all your passion and prayer and muscle and intelligence—and that you love your neighbor as well as you do yourself."

"Good answer!" said Jesus. "Do it and you'll live."

Looking for a loophole, he asked, "And just how would you define 'neighbor'?"

Jesus answered by telling a story. "There was once a man traveling from Jerusalem to Jericho. On the way he was attacked by robbers. They took his clothes, beat him up, and went off leaving him half-dead. Luckily, a priest was on his way down the same road, but when he saw him he angled across to the other side. Then a Levite religious man showed up; he also avoided the injured man.

"A Samaritan traveling the road came on him. When he saw the man's condition, his heart went out to him. He gave him first aid, disinfecting and bandaging his wounds. Then he lifted him onto his donkey, led him to an inn, and made him comfortable. In the morning he took out two silver coins and gave them to the innkeeper, saying, 'Take good care of him. If it costs any more, put it on my bill—I'll pay you on my way back.'

"What do you think? **Which of the three became a neighbor to the man attacked by robbers?**"

"The one who treated him kindly," the religion scholar responded.

Jesus said, "Go and do the same."

THINK "Which of the three became a neighbor to the man attacked by robbers?"

- What is your immediate response to this question?
- Why do you think you responded in this way?
- How familiar are you with this story? Use a scale of 1 to 10 with 1 being "Never heard it" and 10 being "If I had a dime for every time . . ."
- What does Jesus give as a definition of neighborliness?
- Think about this description: "When he saw the man's condition, his heart went out to him." The priest and the Levite let their feet carry them away. The Samaritan let his heart carry him in. Who do you tend to be more like, the Samaritan or the Levite? Why do you think that is?

READ

From *To Kill a Mockingbird*, by Harper Lee[1]

Scout (the narrator) and Jem—sister and brother—have just been saved from harm thanks to the intervention of Boo Radley. In the following scene, Scout is taking Boo—whose real name is Arthur—back to his house, where he had lived a cloistered existence.

I led him to the front porch, where his uneasy steps halted. He was still holding my hand and he gave no sign of letting me go.

"Will you take me home?"

He almost whispered it, in the voice of a child afraid of the dark.

I put my foot on the top step and stopped. I would lead him through our house, but I would never lead him home.

"Mr. Arthur, bend your arm down here, like that. That's right, sir."

I slipped my hand into the crook of his arm. . . .

We came to the street light on the corner, and I wondered how many times Dill had stood there hugging the fat pole, watching, waiting, hoping. I wondered how many times Jem and I had made this journey, but I entered the Radley front gate for the second time in my life. Boo and I walked up the steps to the front porch. His fingers found the front doorknob. He gently released my hand, opened the door, went inside, and shut the door behind him. I never saw him again.

Neighbors bring food with death and flowers with sickness and little things in between. Boo was our neighbor. He gave us two soap dolls, a broken watch and chain, a pair of good-luck pennies, and our lives. But neighbors give in return. We never put back into the tree what we took out of it: we had given him nothing, and it made me sad.

THINK "Which of the three became a neighbor to the man attacked by robbers?"

- Scout defines a neighbor with this statement: "But neighbors give in return." What do you think of her perspective?
- Think about this: Boo Radley takes on a "Good Samaritan" role in Lee's story, saving Jem and Scout from harm. And like the Samaritan to the wounded man, he gives Jem and Scout many things, the most important being their "lives." Who are the Good Samaritans or the Boo Radleys in your life?
- Have any of them given you anything? Have you given anything in return? If so, what? If not, does it in any way make you "sad"?

READ

From *Insearch*, by James Hillman[2]

The cure of the shadow is on the one hand a moral problem, that is, recognition of what we have repressed, how we perform our repressions, how we rationalize and deceive ourselves, what sort of goals we have and what we have hurt, even maimed, in the name of these goals. On the other hand, the cure of the shadow is a problem of love. How far can our love extend to the broken and ruined parts of ourselves, the disgusting and perverse? How much charity and compassion have we for our own inner weakness and sickness? How far can we build an inner society on the principle of love, allowing a place for everyone? And I use the term "cure of the shadow" to emphasize the importance of love. . . .

Loving oneself is no easy matter just because it means loving all of oneself, including the shadow where one is inferior and socially so unacceptable. The care one gives this humiliating part is also the cure. More: as the cure depends on care, so does caring sometimes mean nothing more than carrying. The first essential in redemption of the shadow is the ability to carry it along with you, as did the old Puritans, or the Jews in endless exile, daily aware of their sins, watching for the Devil, on guard lest they slip, a long existential trek with a pack of rocks on the back, with no one on whom to unload it and no sure goal at the end. Yet this carrying and caring cannot be programmatic, in order to develop, in order that the inferiority comply with the ego's goals, for this is hardly love.

Loving the shadow may begin with carrying it, but even that is not enough. At one moment something else must break through, that laughing insight at the paradox of one's own folly which is also everyman's. Then may come the joyful acceptance of the rejected and inferior, a going with it and even a partial living of it. This love may even lead to an identification with and acting-out of the shadow, falling into its fascination. Therefore the moral dimension can never be abandoned. Thus cure is a paradox requiring two incommensurables: the moral recognition that these parts of me are burdensome and intolerable and must change, and the loving, laughing acceptance which takes them just as they are, joyfully, forever.

THINK   "Which of the three became a neighbor to the man attacked by robbers?"

- Think about this: There are the Samaritan-Boo Radley type people out there (external to us; literal neighbors) and there are also the Samaritan-Boo Radley type people within ourselves (internal). And Jesus told the religion scholar to "love your neighbor as well as you do yourself." Go back and read Hillman's words with those thoughts in mind.

- Hillman calls these less acceptable places within ourselves the "shadow." Take some time to think about some of your shadow places, those "broken and ruined parts of ourselves, the disgusting and perverse," where there is "weakness and sickness." Write them down.

- What is your response to Hillman's words? Is this just psychobabble, innerchildishness? Or might he be on to something?

- Hillman advocates a stance of love toward these shadowy neighbors within ourselves—love, imagine that! What might it look like for you to love yourself as you love your neighbor?

READ

From *Care of the Soul*, by Thomas Moore[3]

Taking an interest in the soul is a way of loving it. The ultimate cure, as many ancient and modern psychologies of depth have asserted, comes from love and not from logic. Understanding doesn't take us very far in this work, but love, expressed in patient and careful attention, draws the soul in from its dispersion in problems and fascinations. It has often been noted that most, if not all, problems brought to therapists are issues of love. It makes sense then that the cure is also love.

Taking an interest in one's own soul requires a certain amount of space for reflection and appreciation. Ordinarily we are so identified with movements of the psyche that we can't stand back and take a good look at them. A little distance allows us to see the dynamics among the many elements that make up the life of the soul. By becoming interested in these phenomena, we begin to see our own complexity. Usually we feel that complexity as it hits us unawares from outside, in a multitude of problems and in confusion. If we knew the soul better, we might be ready for the conflicts of life. I often have the sense, when someone tells me anxiously about some knot they find themselves in, that what they perceive as an impossible and painful situation calling for professional intervention is simply the complexity of human life once again manifesting itself. Most of us bring to everyday life a somewhat naive psychological attitude in our expectations that our lives and relationships will be simple. Love of the soul asks for some appreciation for its complexity.

Often care of the soul means not taking sides when there is a conflict at a deep level. It may be necessary to stretch the heart wide enough to embrace contradiction and paradox.

THINK "Which of the three became a neighbor to the
man attacked by robbers?"

- Go back through Moore's excerpt and substitute the word
  neighborhood in place of *soul*.
- With that change in mind, what is your reaction to this passage?
- Ponder these statements: "The ultimate cure, as many ancient
  and modern psychologies of depth have asserted, comes from
  love and not from logic." "Often care of the soul means not
  taking sides when there is a conflict at a deep level. It may be
  necessary to stretch the heart wide enough to embrace contradiction and paradox." What is your reaction to these ideas?
- What does it look like to be a neighbor, according to this
  excerpt?

PRAY

Look back at the "Think" sections. Ruminate on your responses. Let them distill into a prayer, and then write that prayer below.

You know me inside and out . . .

The issue of prayer is not prayer; the issue of prayer is God.

ABRAHAM HESCHEL

LIVE　　　"Which of the three became a neighbor to the man
attacked by robbers?"

The challenge now is to take this question further along—to live out
this question. Think of one thing, *just one*, that you can personally
do to wrestle with the question, inhabit the character of it, and live
it in everyday life. In the following space, jot down your thoughts on
this "one thing." Read the quotes that follow for additional inspiration. During the coming week, pray about this "one thing," talk with a
close friend about it, and learn to live the question.

One thing . . .

With thinking we may be beside ourselves in a sane sense.
　　　　　　　　　　　　　　　Henry David Thoreau

Who are the people in your neighborhood? . . .
They're the people that you meet
When you're walking down the street

They're the people that you meet each day!
　　　　　　　　　　　　　　Song from *Sesame Street*

Live the questions now. Perhaps you will then gradually, without
noticing it, live along some distant day into the answer.
　　　　　RAINER MARIA RILKE, *LETTERS TO A YOUNG POET*

"And don't you think the Father who conceived you in love will give the Holy Spirit when you ask him?" (Luke 11:13)

Before You Begin

Take some time to reflect and prepare your heart and mind for this study. Read the following Scripture passage. Soak up God's Word. There's no hurry. Then, when you're ready, turn the page and begin.

MATTHEW 6:9-13

> Our Father in heaven,
> Reveal who you are.
> Set the world right;
> Do what's best—
>   as above, so below.
> Keep us alive with three square meals.
> Keep us forgiven with you and forgiving others.
> Keep us safe from ourselves and the Devil.
> You're in charge!
> You can do anything you want!
> You're ablaze in beauty!
>   Yes. Yes. Yes.

READ

LUKE 11:1-13

One day he was praying in a certain place. When he finished, one of his disciples said, "Master, teach us to pray just as John taught his disciples."

So he said, "When you pray, say,

Father,
Reveal who you are.
Set the world right.
Keep us alive with three square meals.
Keep us forgiven with you and forgiving others.
Keep us safe from ourselves and the Devil."

Then he said, "Imagine what would happen if you went to a friend in the middle of the night and said, 'Friend, lend me three loaves of bread. An old friend traveling through just showed up, and I don't have a thing on hand.'

"The friend answers from his bed, 'Don't bother me. The door's locked; my children are all down for the night; I can't get up to give you anything.'

"But let me tell you, even if he won't get up because he's a friend, if you stand your ground, knocking and waking all the neighbors, he'll finally get up and get you whatever you need.

"Here's what I'm saying:

Ask and you'll get;
Seek and you'll find;
Knock and the door will open.

"Don't bargain with God. Be direct. Ask for what you need. This is not a cat-and-mouse, hide-and-seek game we're in. If your little boy asks for a serving of fish, do you scare him with a live snake on his plate? If your little girl asks for an egg, do you trick her with a spider? As bad as you are, you wouldn't think of such a thing—you're at least decent to your own children. **And don't you think the Father who conceived you in love will give the Holy Spirit when you ask him?"**

THINK   *"And don't you think the Father who conceived you in love will give the Holy Spirit when you ask him?"*

- What is your immediate response to this question?
- Why do you think you responded in this way?
- If you had to choose a word to describe the theme of this passage, what would it be? Why?
- Write down some words or phrases that speak to you.
- Think about the last time you played a cat-and-mouse game with God. What was the issue? Why were you indirect with the Father?
- Does that describe the way you usually interact with God in prayer? If so, think about why that is. Don't try to find an answer yet; let that one simmer.

READ

From *Working the Angles*, by Eugene H. Peterson[1]

Prayer is not something we think up to get God's attention or enlist his favor. Prayer is *answering* speech. The first word is God's word. Prayer is a human word and is never the first word, never the primary word, never the initiating and shaping word simply because *we* are never first, never primary. We do not honor prayer by treating it as something that it is not, even when that something is, as we suppose, sacred and exalted. What we do, in fact, is make prayer into a verbal idol. It then becomes a tool that works our diminishment and maybe even our damnation. . . . We must develop within ourselves the means for a full and continuous awareness of its secondary quality, its *answering* character. Otherwise we drift unaware into verbal idolatry and its consequent diminishments. We require repeated and forceful reminders: the first word is everywhere and always God's word to us, not ours to him. Vigilant attentiveness is necessary to keep our weapons sharp against these barbarian prayers that are requested and preferred by nearly everyone we meet. . . .

Prayer is language used to respond to the most that has been said to us, with the potential for saying all that is in us. Prayer is the development of speech into maturity, language in process of being adequate to answer the one who has spoken most comprehensively to us, namely, God. Put this way, it is clear that prayer is not a narrow use of language for special occasions but the broadest use of language into which everything that is truly human in us . . . comes to expression.

THINK   "And don't you think the Father who conceived you in love will give the Holy Spirit when you ask him?"

- Although Peterson's words are aimed at pastors, they have benefit for us all. What are your impressions after reading this passage?

- Take a minute to ponder the following words: "Prayer is not something we think up to get God's attention or enlist his favor. Prayer is *answering* speech." What do you think about this?
- Have you ever considered prayer as "answering speech"?
- What is Peterson talking about when he writes, "the most that has been said to us"? What are we responding to?

READ

Jeremiah 31:2-6

This is the way GOD put it:

"They found grace out in the desert,
    these people who survived the killing.
Israel, out looking for a place to rest,
    met God out looking for them!"
GOD told them, "I've never quit loving you and never will.
    Expect love, love, and more love!
And so now I'll start over with you and build you up again,
    dear virgin Israel.
You'll resume your singing,
    grabbing tambourines and joining the dance.
You'll go back to your old work of planting vineyards
    on the Samaritan hillsides,
And sit back and enjoy the fruit—
    oh, how you'll enjoy those harvests!"

Ephesians 1:3-6,11-12

How blessed is God! And what a blessing he is! He's the Father of our Master, Jesus Christ, and takes us to the high places of blessing in him. Long before he laid down earth's foundations, he had us in mind, had settled on us as the focus of his love, to be made whole and holy by his love. Long, long ago he decided to adopt us into his family through Jesus Christ. (What pleasure he took in planning this!) He wanted us to enter into the celebration of his lavish gift-giving by the hand of his beloved Son. . . .

It's in Christ that we find out who we are and what we are living for. Long before we first heard of Christ and got our hopes up, he had his eye on us, had designs on us for glorious living, part of the overall purpose he is working out in everything and everyone.

THINK "And don't you think the Father who conceived you in love will give the Holy Spirit when you ask him?"

- How do these passages make you feel?
- What do you hear in them as "the most that has been said to us," that which we are answering in our prayers?
- Let the following phrases settle deep within your heart:

"I've never quit loving you and never will."

"Expect love, love, and more love!"

"Long before he laid down earth's foundations, he had us in mind, had settled on us as the focus of his love, to be made whole and holy by his love."

READ

From *Listening to Your Life*, by Frederick Buechner[2]

In the Episcopal Order of Worship, the priest sometimes introduces the Lord's Prayer with the words, "Now, as our Savior Christ hath taught us, we are bold to say, . . ." The word *bold* is worth thinking about. We do well not to pray the prayer lightly. It takes guts to pray it at all. We can pray it in the unthinking and perfunctory way we usually do only by disregarding what we are saying.

"Thy will be done" is what we are saying. That is the climax of the first half of the prayer. We are asking God to be God. We are asking God to do not what we want but what God wants. We are asking God to make manifest the holiness that is now mostly hidden, to set free in all its terrible splendor the devastating power that is now mostly under restraint. "Thy kingdom come . . . on earth" is what we are saying. And if that were suddenly to happen, what then? What would stand and what would fall? Who would be welcomed in and who would be thrown the Hell out? Which if any of our most precious visions of what God is and of what human beings are would prove to be more or less on the mark and which would turn out to be phony as three-dollar bills? Boldness indeed. To speak these words is to invite the tiger out of the cage, to unleash a power that makes atomic power look like a warm breeze.

You need to be bold in another way to speak the second half. Give us. Forgive us. Don't test us. Deliver us. If it takes guts to face the omnipotence that is God's, it takes perhaps no less to face the impotence that is ours. We can do nothing without God. Without God we are nothing.

It is only the words "Our Father" that make the prayer bearable. If God is indeed something like a father, then as something like children maybe we can risk approaching him anyway.

THINK

"And don't you think the Father who conceived you in love will give the Holy Spirit when you ask him?"

- Do you agree with Buechner? Why or why not?
- How does the following sentence make you feel: "It is only the words 'Our Father' that make the prayer bearable"?
- If you can be so bold, what is it that you would like to ask "the Father who conceived you in love" for right now? Remember, "Don't bargain with God. Be direct. Ask for what you need. This is not a cat-and-mouse, hide-and-seek game we're in."

PRAY

Look back at the "Think" sections. Ruminate on your responses. Let them distill into a prayer, and then write that prayer below.

My Father . . .

The issue of prayer is not prayer; the issue of prayer is God.

ABRAHAM HESCHEL

LIVE   "And don't you think the Father who conceived you in
love will give the Holy Spirit when you ask him?"

The challenge now is to take this question further along—to live out
this question. Think of one thing, *just one*, that you can personally
do to wrestle with the question, inhabit the character of it, and live
it in everyday life. In the following space, jot down your thoughts on
this "one thing." Read the quotes that follow for additional inspiration. During the coming week, pray about this "one thing," talk with a
close friend about it, and learn to live the question.

One thing . . .

So if you are asked, "Who is a Christian?" the best answer you
can give is, "A Christian is none other than someone who has
learned to pray the Lord's Prayer."

William H. Willimon and Stanley M. Hauerwas

This prayer starts by addressing God intimately and lovingly,
as "Father"—and by bowing before his greatness and majesty.
If you can hold those two together, you're already on the way
to understanding what Christianity is all about.

N. T. Wright

Live the questions now. Perhaps you will then gradually, without
noticing it, live along some distant day into the answer.

RAINER MARIA RILKE, *LETTERS TO A YOUNG POET*

"True, they can kill you, but *then* what can they do?"
(Luke 12:4)

Before You Begin

Take some time to reflect and prepare your heart and mind
for this study. Read the following Scripture passage. Soak
up God's Word. There's no hurry. Then, when you're ready,
turn the page and begin.

1 Corinthians 15:54-57

Then the saying will come true:

> Death swallowed by triumphant Life!
> Who got the last word, oh, Death?
> Oh, Death, who's afraid of you now?

It was sin that made death so frightening and law-code
guilt that gave sin its leverage, its destructive power. But
now in a single victorious stroke of Life, all three—sin,
guilt, death—are gone, the gift of our Master, Jesus Christ.
Thank God!

READ

Luke 12:1-10

By this time the crowd, unwieldy and stepping on each other's toes, numbered into the thousands. But Jesus' primary concern was his disciples. He said to them, "Watch yourselves carefully so you don't get contaminated with Pharisee yeast, Pharisee phoniness. You can't keep your true self hidden forever; before long you'll be exposed. You can't hide behind a religious mask forever; sooner or later the mask will slip and your true face will be known. You can't whisper one thing in private and preach the opposite in public; the day's coming when those whispers will be repeated all over town.

"I'm speaking to you as dear friends. Don't be bluffed into silence or insincerity by the threats of religious bullies. **True, they can kill you, but *then* what can they do?** There's nothing they can do to your soul, your core being. Save your fear for God, who holds your entire life—body and soul—in his hands.

"What's the price of two or three pet canaries? Some loose change, right? But God never overlooks a single one. And he pays even greater attention to you, down to the last detail—even numbering the hairs on your head! So don't be intimidated by all this bully talk. You're worth more than a million canaries.

"Stand up for me among the people you meet and the Son of Man will stand up for you before all God's angels. But if you pretend you don't know me, do you think I'll defend you before God's angels?

"If you bad-mouth the Son of Man out of misunderstanding or ignorance, that can be overlooked. But if you're knowingly attacking God himself, taking aim at the Holy Spirit, that won't be overlooked."

THINK

"True, they can kill you, but *then* what can they do?"

- What is your immediate response to this question?
- Why do you think you responded in this way?
- As you think about this passage, remember that "Jesus' primary concern was his disciples." What feelings does this passage evoke in you?
- Think about this sentence: "Don't be bluffed into silence or insincerity by the threats of religious bullies." Do you know anyone who has been bluffed? Describe the situation and the outcome; did he or she become silent or insincere?

READ

From *Fahrenheit 451*, by Ray Bradbury[1]

The front door opened slowly. Faber peered out, looking very old in the light and very fragile and very much afraid. The old man looked as if he had not been out of the house in years. He and the white plaster walls inside were much the same. There was white in the flesh of his mouth and his cheeks and his hair was white and his eyes had faded, with white in the vague blueness there. Then his eyes touched on the book under Montag's arm and he did not look so old any more and not quite as fragile. Slowly, his fear went.

"I'm sorry. One has to be careful."

He looked at the book under Montag's arm and could not stop. "So it's true."

Montag stepped inside. The door shut.

"Sit down." Faber backed up, as if he feared the book might vanish if he took his eyes from it. Behind him, the door to a bedroom stood open, and in that room a litter of machinery and steel tools were strewn upon a desktop. Montag had only a glimpse, before Faber, seeing Montag's attention diverted, turned quickly and shut the bedroom door and stood holding the knob with a trembling hand. His gaze returned unsteadily to Montag, who was now seated with the book in his lap. "The book—where did you—?"

"I stole it."

Faber, for the first time, raised his eyes and looked directly into Montag's face. "You're brave."

"No," said Montag. "My wife's dying. A friend of mine's already dead. Someone who may have been a friend was burnt less than twenty-four hours ago. You're the only one I knew might help me. To see. To see . . ."

Faber's hands itched on his knees. "May I?"

"It's been a long time. I'm not a religious man. But it's been a long time." Faber turned the pages, stopping here and there to read. "It's as good as I remember. Lord, how they've changed it in our 'parlors' these days. Christ is one of the 'family' now. I often wonder if God recognizes his own son the way we've dressed him up, or is it dressed him down? He's a regular peppermint stick now, all sugar-crystal and saccharine when he isn't making veiled references to certain commercial products that every worshiper *absolutely* needs." Faber sniffed the book. "Do you know that books smell like nutmeg or some spice from a foreign land? I loved to smell them when I was a boy. Lord, there were a lot of lovely books once, before we let them go." Faber turned the pages. "Mr. Montag, you are looking at a coward. I saw the way things were going, a long time back. I said nothing. I'm one of the innocents who could have spoken up and out when no one would listen to the 'guilty,' but I did not speak and thus became guilty myself. And when finally they set the structure to burn the books, using the firemen, I grunted a few times and subsided, for there were no others grunting or yelling with me, by then. Now it's too late." Faber closed the Bible.

THINK "True, they can kill you, but *then* what can they do?"

- Mr. Faber had experienced a kind of religious bullying. And you read his outcome: "Mr. Montag, you are looking at a coward. I saw the way things were going, a long time back. I said nothing." Have there been times when you saw the way things were going, the religious bullying, and yet said nothing? If not, fine. Don't manufacture a scenario. But if you've had any church/religious experience at all, there was probably a moment when you were "bluffed into silence." Write about this memory.

- Mr. Faber continues, "I'm one of the innocents who could have spoken up and out when no one would listen to the 'guilty,' but I did not speak and thus became guilty myself." Mr. Faber was "contaminated with Pharisee yeast." What about the memory you wrote down? Would you describe it as contamination?

• Read again his final haunting words: "I grunted a few times and subsided, for there were no others grunting or yelling with me, by then. Now it's too late." Mr. Faber resigned himself to "insincerity" and cowardice. What do you think would have happened to you if you had spoken up instead of being silent? Write down what comes to mind.

READ

"There Are Men Too Gentle to Live Among Wolves," by James Kavanaugh[2]

> There are men too gentle to live among wolves
> Who prey upon them with IBM eyes
> And sell their hearts and guts for martinis at noon.
> There are men too gentle for a savage world
> Who dream instead of snow and children and Halloween
> And wonder if the leaves will change their color soon.
>
> There are men too gentle to live among wolves
> Who anoint them for burial with greedy claws
> And murder them for a merchant's profit and gain.
> There are men too gentle for a corporate world
> Who dream instead of candied apples and ferris wheels
> And pause to hear the distant whistle of a train.
>
> There are men too gentle to live among wolves
> Who devour them with eager appetite and search
> For other men to prey upon and suck their childhood dry.
> There are men too gentle for an accountant's world
> Who dream instead of Easter eggs and fragrant grass
> And search for beauty in the mystery of the sky.
>
> There are men too gentle to live among wolves
> Who toss them like a lost and wounded dove.
> Such gentle men are lonely in a merchant's world,
> Unless they have a gentle one to love.

THINK   "True, they can kill you, but *then* what can they do?"

- Although Kavanaugh speaks of a gentle man or person, it is tempered by the reality of this "merchant's world." Go back through the poem and list what the religious bullies can do to you.

- This may seem like a poem about finding your inner child, but instead, think of it as *becoming* like a child. Remember, "Unless you accept God's kingdom in the simplicity of a child, you'll never get in" (Mark 10:15). With this view of Kavanaugh's words, what is your response to the poem?

- In what ways do you see Jesus as a "gentle one"? How does this role impact the way you relate to Jesus? To the world around you?

READ

Hebrews 11:13-16,33-38

Each one of these people of faith died not yet having in hand what was promised, but still believing. How did they do it? They saw it way off in the distance, waved their greeting, and accepted the fact that they were transients in this world. People who live this way make it plain that they are looking for their true home. If they were homesick for the old country, they could have gone back any time they wanted. But they were after a far better country than that—*heaven* country. You can see why God is so proud of them, and has a City waiting for them. . . .

Through acts of faith, they toppled kingdoms, made justice work, took the promises for themselves. They were protected from lions, fires, and sword thrusts, turned disadvantage to advantage, won battles, routed alien armies. Women received their loved ones back from the dead. There were those who, under torture, refused to give in and go free, preferring something better: resurrection. Others braved abuse and whips, and, yes, chains and dungeons. We have stories of those who were stoned, sawed in two, murdered in cold blood; stories of vagrants wandering the earth in animal skins, homeless, friendless, powerless—the world didn't deserve them!—making their way as best they could on the cruel edges of the world.

THINK "True, they can kill you, but *then* what can they do?"

- Like Kavanaugh, the writer of Hebrews lists many things the religious bullies did to those "looking for their true home." Think about these words for a moment: torture, abuse, whips, chains, dungeons, stoned, sawed, murdered, homeless, friendless, and powerless. Do you see how the love of a gentle One is essential in this life? How does that make you feel?
- Have you ever considered yourself a "transient in this world"? What images does the word *transient* bring to mind?

- Do the truths from Hebrews 11 redeem the word *transient* in any way for you?
- Would you describe yourself as a person faithfully looking for a "better country"? Explain.

PRAY

Look back at the "Think" sections. Ruminate on your responses.
Let them distill into a prayer, and then write that prayer below.

Gentle One . . .

The issue of prayer is not prayer; the issue of prayer is God.
ABRAHAM HESCHEL

LIVE

"True, they can kill you, but *then* what can they do?"

The challenge now is to take this question further along—to live out this question. Think of one thing, *just one*, that you can personally do to wrestle with the question, inhabit the character of it, and live it in everyday life. In the following space, jot down your thoughts on this "one thing." Read the quotes that follow for additional inspiration. During the coming week, pray about this "one thing," talk with a close friend about it, and learn to live the question.

One thing . . .

No nation, no social institution, ever acquired coherence without some sort of fight. Out of the fight come its myths and its heroes.

Thurman Arnold

Home is a notion that only the nations of the homeless fully appreciate and only the uprooted comprehend.

Wallace Stegner

Live the questions now. Perhaps you will then gradually, without noticing it, live along some distant day into the answer.

RAINER MARIA RILKE, *LETTERS TO A YOUNG POET*

LESSON 7

"Do you think I came to smooth things over and make everything nice?" (Luke 12:51)

Before You Begin

Take some time to reflect and prepare your heart and mind for this study. Read the following Scripture passage. Soak up God's Word. There's no hurry. Then, when you're ready, turn the page and begin.

Luke 14:25-27

One day when large groups of people were walking along with him, Jesus turned and told them, "Anyone who comes to me but refuses to let go of father, mother, spouse, children, brothers, sisters—yes, even one's own self!—can't be my disciple. Anyone who won't shoulder his own cross and follow behind me can't be my disciple."

READ

Luke 12:42-59

The Master said, "Let me ask you: Who is the dependable manager, full of common sense, that the master puts in charge of his staff to feed them well and on time? He is a blessed man if when the master shows up he's doing his job. But if he says to himself, 'The master is certainly taking his time,' begins maltreating the servants and maids, throws parties for his friends, and gets drunk, the master will walk in when he least expects it, give him the thrashing of his life, and put him back in the kitchen peeling potatoes.

"The servant who knows what his master wants and ignores it, or insolently does whatever he pleases, will be thoroughly thrashed. But if he does a poor job through ignorance, he'll get off with a slap on the hand. Great gifts mean great responsibilities; greater gifts, greater responsibilities!

"I've come to start a fire on this earth — how I wish it were blazing right now! I've come to change everything, turn everything rightside up — how I long for it to be finished! **Do you think I came to smooth things over and make everything nice?** Not so. I've come to disrupt and confront! From now on, when you find five in a house, it will be —

Three against two,
    and two against three;
Father against son,
    and son against father;
Mother against daughter,
    and daughter against mother;
Mother-in-law against bride,
    and bride against mother-in-law."

Then he turned to the crowd: "When you see clouds coming in from the west, you say, 'Storm's coming' — and you're right.

And when the wind comes out of the south, you say, 'This'll be a hot one'—and you're right. Frauds! You know how to tell a change in the weather, so don't tell me you can't tell a change in the season, the God-season we're in right now.

"You don't have to be a genius to understand these things. Just use your common sense, the kind you'd use if, while being taken to court, you decided to settle up with your accuser on the way, knowing that if the case went to the judge you'd probably go to jail and pay every last penny of the fine. That's the kind of decision I'm asking you to make."

THINK   "Do you think I came to smooth things over and make everything nice?"

- What is your immediate response to this question?
- Why do you think you responded in this way?
- What words or phrases in this passage speak to you?
- How would you describe a "servant who knows what his master wants"?
- Jesus very clearly states, "I've come to disrupt and confront!" What do those words mean to you?
- Of all the examples of people being "against" each other, Jesus chose to use family members (father, son, mother, daughter, and so forth). Why do you think he chose these examples?

READ

From *The Awakened Heart*, by Gerald G. May, MD[1]

The real problem with habit patterns, in families and other institutions as well, is that the most ingrained habits are addictions. Tradition or dysfunction, daily routine or entrenched expectation, our most frozen habits fill up our spaces and limit our freedom for love. Just as love and grace can be astronomically expanded in community, the addictions of family and institution can be more treacherous, more insidious, and more malignant than anything an individual mind might dream up. And the addictions are more deeply entrenched. Prevent the pattern and the whole group goes into withdrawal symptoms. Let one person seek freedom, and the whole system can collude to undermine it. And nearly always it goes on unconsciously.

I have never understood all the theory about codependence and dysfunctionality in families, but the theory clearly has its finger on something real. Families, like institutions, do become addicted to destructive patterns of behavior and relationship. Collectively, we become addicted more powerfully, deeply, and rapidly than we do as individuals. And if we cannot free ourselves from our individual addictions without intervening grace, we certainly cannot liberate our families and institutions by the power of will alone.

The terms are not important. Whether you call it dependence or codependence, compulsive collusion or being a slave of love, it happens when love loses its freedom to addiction.

THINK   "Do you think I came to smooth things over and make everything nice?"

- What do you think of May's words?
- Take some time to think about the habit patterns of your family while you were growing up. List as many as you can.

- Now determine which ones were traditional and which were dysfunctional. We're not trying to establish hard and fast categories here; we're simply seeking the benefit of reflection.
- Can you recall a time when a pattern was prevented and the whole group went into withdrawal? Or maybe one person sought freedom and the group colluded to undermine it?
- Think about May's last few words: "when love loses its freedom."

READ

From *The Four Loves*, by C. S. Lewis[2]

As so often, Our Lord's own words are both far fiercer and far more tolerable than those of the theologians. He says nothing about guarding against earthly loves for fear we might be hurt; He says something that cracks like a whip about trampling them all under foot the moment they hold us back from following Him. "If any man come to me and hate not his father and mother and wife . . . and his own life also, he cannot be my disciple" (Luke XIV, 26).

But how are we to understand the word *hate*? That Love Himself should be commanding what we ordinarily mean by hatred—commanding us to cherish resentment, to gloat over another's misery, to delight in injuring him—is almost a contradiction in terms. I think Our Lord, in the sense here intended, "hated" St. Peter when he said, "Get thee behind me." To hate is to reject, to set one's face against, to make no concession to, the Beloved when the Beloved utters, however sweetly and however pitiably, the suggestions of the Devil. A man, said Jesus, who tries to serve two masters, will "hate" the one and "love" the other. It is not, surely, mere feelings of aversion and liking that are here in question. He will adhere to, consent to, work for, the one and not for the other. Consider again, "I loved Jacob and I *hated* Esau" (Malachi I, 2-3). How is the thing called God's "hatred" of Esau displayed in the actual story? Not at all as we might expect. There is of course no ground for assuming that Esau made a bad end and was a lost soul; the Old Testament, here as elsewhere, has nothing to say about such matters. And, from all we are told, Esau's earthly life was, in every ordinary sense, a good deal more blessed than Jacob's. It is Jacob who has all the disappointments, humiliations, terrors, and bereavements. But he has something which Esau has not. He is a patriarch. He hands on the Hebraic tradition, transmits the vocation and the blessing, becomes an ancestor of Our Lord. The "loving" of Jacob seems to mean the acceptance of Jacob for a high (and painful) vocation; the "hating" of Esau, his rejection. He is "turned down," fails to "make the grade," is found useless for the purpose. So, in the last resort, we must turn down or disqualify our nearest and dearest when they come between us and our obedience to God. Heaven knows, it will seem to them sufficiently like hatred. We must not act on the pity we feel; we must be blind to tears and deaf to pleadings.

I will not say that this duty is hard; some find it too easy; some, hard almost beyond endurance. What is hard for all is to know when the occasion for such "hating" has arisen. Our temperaments deceive us.

THINK   "Do you think I came to smooth things over and make everything nice?"

- What do you think of Lewis's distinctions of the word *hate*?
- "So, in the last resort, we must turn down or disqualify our nearest and dearest when they come between us and our obedience to God." Have you had an experience like this? Describe it. Was it hard? Too easy? Almost beyond endurance?
- Did it seem to the person or people rejected "sufficiently like hatred"? What was the response?
- Don't miss Lewis's last statement: "What is hard for all is to know when the occasion for such 'hating' has arisen. Our temperaments deceive us." Did your temperament deceive you in your experience? Explain.

READ

From *The River Why*, by David James Duncan[3]

When a young Tillamook was ready for manhood, he was led to a fire by the elders. He was made naked. His boyhood name was taken and burned. The people of his village then closed round him like trees round a clearing. He was given a blanket, a knife, and a pine knot. The pine knot was lit. He took the knot and departed; his people sang him away.

The Tillamook lit his fire and huddled down beside it. Then he waited. The night came on. He paid it no heed. He knew he'd be waiting a long time. He'd nothing to eat. He'd no clothes but a blanket. He felt the cold, the hunger, the loneliness. He knew he'd be feeling these things. These things were not important now. He had come to meet them, to journey past them. . . .

The Tillamook, with his pine knot, went to no source. He had been told by his elders that the source was everywhere, so he made his encampment on the first waters he found once the knot burned dim. Then he waited, naked as a winter tree, to make his elders' words come true.

By night he kept his fire going. By day he rested in sunlight, rain or shadow. Twice daily he would bathe in the icy water, scrubbing his flesh with evergreen boughs. The boughs hurt, he was weak, and the water was bitter cold. But hurt, weakness, and cold were none of them the one he waited for. He let them do their work. They left him in peace.

For three, four, maybe five days the Tillamook waited. If the waiting grew very long, his people came to find him. All of them came, filling the woods with chatter. When he was found, they gathered a little distance downstream. Then they just stood there, peering, craning their necks, calling to him, laughing or crying—whichever might work best—begging him to come home. . . .

But he raved at them. He threw rocks at them, reviled them, drove them all away, just as they hoped he would. They knew that they were not the one he waited for. They knew that his long wait was the sign of a powerful spirit's approach. They knew, when he hurled stones at them, that he had not grown sick or feebleminded. They left him in peace.

He waited alone. . . . The young Tillamook grew still.

Because he stayed still, the animals began to come. For days they had watched him. For days he had taken no notice. From the fasting and bathing his scent had grown faint, and from the long wait it had become familiar. . . . Maybe this Tillamook had become a kind of tree. Maybe he had become a spirit. . . .

But in the end, the one for whom he waited came. Crept up in silence, with all its power sheathed—yet the motionless boy knew, and his heart danced. His spirit-helper had come!

The spirit made no sound, yet the boy could hear it—and its voice was kind, for he had waited well. It told the boy his man-name, and it told him his true name. It told him what his life's work would be. And, whether boat-builder, wood-carver, hunter, shaman, fisherman or chief, it promised him help, and told how that help could be summoned.

THINK   "Do you think I came to smooth things over and make everything nice?"

- What if we all had to make some kind of break with family, friends, and home in order to go and wait for the One, the Holy Spirit, to come? What if this was an extremely difficult, harsh, and disruptive undertaking? What if, without this journey, we would never learn our true names? Just think about it.
- What words or phrases spoke to you as you read of the young Tillamook? Why?
- Are you waiting well? Are you allowing your children to wait well? What feels cold, hungry, and lonely may just be the path to a heart that can dance!

THINK (continued)

PRAY

Look back at the "Think" sections. Ruminate on your responses. Let them distill into a prayer, and then write that prayer below.

Great Spirit . . .

The issue of prayer is not prayer; the issue of prayer is God.

ABRAHAM HESCHEL

LIVE   "Do you think I came to smooth things over and make everything nice?"

The challenge now is to take this question further along—to live out this question. Think of one thing, *just one*, that you can personally do to wrestle with the question, inhabit the character of it, and live it in everyday life. In the following space, jot down your thoughts on this "one thing." Read the quotes that follow for additional inspiration. During the coming week, pray about this "one thing," talk with a close friend about it, and learn to live the question.

One thing . . .

for every real lock
there is only one real key . . .
it's the key to the one real door
it opens the river and the sky both at once

W. S. Merwin

Live the questions now. Perhaps you will then gradually, without noticing it, live along some distant day into the answer.
RAINER MARIA RILKE, *LETTERS TO A YOUNG POET*

"Wouldn't you leave the ninety-nine in the wilderness and go after the lost one until you found it?" (Luke 15:4)

Before You Begin

Take some time to reflect and prepare your heart and mind for this study. Read the following Scripture passage. Soak up God's Word. There's no hurry. Then, when you're ready, turn the page and begin.

Matthew 28:18-20

Jesus, undeterred, went right ahead and gave his charge: "God authorized and commanded me to commission you: Go out and train everyone you meet, far and near, in this way of life, marking them by baptism in the threefold name: Father, Son, and Holy Spirit. Then instruct them in the practice of all I have commanded you. I'll be with you as you do this, day after day after day, right up to the end of the age."

READ

Luke 15:1-10

By this time a lot of men and women of doubtful reputation were hanging around Jesus, listening intently. The Pharisees and religion scholars were not pleased, not at all pleased. They growled, "He takes in sinners and eats meals with them, treating them like old friends." Their grumbling triggered this story.

"Suppose one of you had a hundred sheep and lost one. **Wouldn't you leave the ninety-nine in the wilderness and go after the lost one until you found it?** When found, you can be sure you would put it across your shoulders, rejoicing, and when you got home call in your friends and neighbors, saying, 'Celebrate with me! I've found my lost sheep!' Count on it—there's more joy in heaven over one sinner's rescued life than over ninety-nine good people in no need of rescue.

"Or imagine a woman who has ten coins and loses one. Won't she light a lamp and scour the house, looking in every nook and cranny until she finds it? And when she finds it you can be sure she'll call her friends and neighbors: 'Celebrate with me! I found my lost coin!' Count on it—that's the kind of party God's angels throw every time one lost soul turns to God."

THINK "Wouldn't you leave the ninety-nine in the wilderness and go after the lost one until you found it?"

- What is your immediate response to this question?
- Why do you think you responded in this way?
- When was the last time you were in a crowd of people of "doubtful reputation"? What was going on?
- How do you act around people of doubtful reputation? Do you treat them like "old friends"?
- In the story, what emotion results from finding the lost sheep and the lost coin?
- How long has it been since you felt that way?

THINK (continued)

READ

From *Of Mice and Men*, by John Steinbeck[1]

Lennie spoke craftily, "Tell me—like you done before."

"Tell you what?"

"About the rabbits."

George snapped, "You ain't gonna put nothing over on me."

Lennie pleaded, "Come on, George. Tell me. Please, George. Like you done before."

"You get a kick outta that, don't you? Awright, I'll tell you, and then we'll eat our supper. . . ."

George's voice became deeper. He repeated his words rhythmically as though he had said them many times before. "Guys like us, that work on ranches, are the loneliest guys in the world. They got no family. They don't belong no place. They come to a ranch an' work up a stake and then they go inta town and blow their stake, and the first thing you know they're poundin' their tail on some other ranch. They ain't got nothing to look ahead to."

Lennie was delighted. "That's it—that's it. Now tell how it is with us."

George went on. "With us it ain't like that. We got a future. We got somebody to talk to. . . . We don't have to sit in no bar room blowin' in our jack jus' because we got no place else to go. If them other guys get in jail they can rot. . . . But not us."

Lennie broke in. *"But not us! An' why? Because . . . because I got you to look after me, and you got me to look after you, and that's why."* He laughed delightedly. "Go on, now, George!"

"You got it by heart. You can do it yourself."

"No, you. I forget some a' the things. Tell about how it's gonna be."

"O.K. Someday—we gonna get the jack together and we're gonna have a little house and a couple of acres an' a cow and some pigs and—"

"An' live off the fatta the lan'," Lennie shouted. "An' have

rabbits. Go on, George! Tell about what we're gonna have in the garden and about the rabbits in the cages and about the rain in the winter and the stove, and how thick the cream is on the milk like you can hardly cut it. Tell about that, George."

THINK   "Wouldn't you leave the ninety-nine in the wilderness and go after the lost one until you found it?"

- Look for parallels between the passage from Luke and Steinbeck's passage. Take your time with this. What do you see?
- If you could choose an emotion to describe the way Lennie listened to George, what would it be?
- Lennie's "lost soul" was turned every time George would tell him about the rabbits, the "good news." You could say he was "found" again. Reflect on this and the spiritual implications in your own life.

READ

From *The Gospel in a Pluralist Society*, by Lesslie Newbigin[2]

We can only understand the biblical teaching about election if we see it as part of the whole way of understanding the human situation which is characteristic of the Bible. Here, in contrast to both the Indian and the modern Western views, there is no attempt to see the human person as an autonomous individual, and the human relation with God as the relation of the alone to the alone. From its very beginning the Bible sees human life in terms of relationships. There is no attempt to strip away the accidents of history in order to find the real essence of what it is to be human. Human life is seen in terms of mutual relationships: first, the most fundamental relation, between man and woman, then between parents and children, then between families and clans and nations. The Bible does not speak about "humanity" but about "all the families of the earth" or "all the nations." It follows that this mutual relatedness, this dependence of one on another, is not merely part of the journey toward the goal of salvation, but is intrinsic to the goal itself. For knowing God, for being in communion with him, we are dependent on the one whom he gives us to be the bearer of this relation, not just as a teacher and guide on the way but as the partner in the end. There is, there can be, no private salvation, no salvation which does not involve us with one another. Therefore, if I may venture to use a metaphor which I have used elsewhere, God's saving revelation of himself does not come to us straight down from above—through the skylight, as we might say. In order to receive God's saving revelation we have to open the door to the neighbor whom he sends as his appointed messenger, and—moreover—to receive that messenger not as a temporary teacher or guide whom we can dispense with when we ourselves have learned what is needed, but as one who will permanently share our home. There is no salvation except one in which we are saved together through the one whom God sends to be the bearer of his salvation.

THINK   "Wouldn't you leave the ninety-nine in the wilderness and go after the lost one until you found it?"

- What do you think about Newbigin's words?
- Who was the one who left the ninety-nine and went after you
  to find you when you were lost? Think about that time in detail.
- How does your salvation experience line up with this statement: "There is no salvation except one in which we are saved
  together"? Do you believe that?
- Consider this: "In order to receive God's saving revelation we
  have to open the door to the neighbor whom he sends as his
  appointed messenger." Can you see how important it is that
  you search for the lost one? What does that mean for you in
  everyday terms?

READ

From *The Celtic Way of Evangelism*, by George G. Hunter III[3]

So the Romans had observed some Celtic peoples historically; indeed, Julius Caesar had even written about them. Furthermore, the Romans had heard many rumors about the Irish Celts. Why did the Romans think of the Celtic peoples, especially the Irish, as "barbarians"? Well, the Romans tended to regard everyone who wasn't culturally Roman as "barbarian"! The Romans regarded literacy as a sure and certain sign of being civilized; the Irish Celts did not read and write and were not interested. The Irish were "emotional" people, volatile personalities known for letting the full range of human emotions get out of control. The Romans virtually equated "being civilized" with emotional control. In warfare "all the Celts . . . stripped before battle and rushed their enemy naked, carrying sword and shield but wearing only sandals and torc—a twisted, golden neck ornament . . . [while] howling and, it seemed, possessed by demons!"[4] (Roman soldiers would have noticed that!) Furthermore, the Celts were known to decapitate some conquered enemy warriors, and to practice human sacrifice in some of their religious rituals. For reasons such as these, the Romans stereotyped the Irish Celts as "barbarians," and therefore probably unreachable. Nevertheless, by Patrick's time there was some interest, especially at the papal level, in the possibility of reaching "barbarians," and that is probably why Patrick's Macedonian vision found support.

One would naturally assume that the British Church, which had ordained Patrick a bishop and sent him to Ireland, would continue to affirm his mission and celebrate its achievements. This was far from the case. The generation of British bishops who succeeded the bishops who originally sent Patrick did not "own" their predecessor's appointment. Some of them, perhaps most, criticized him savagely. This criticism stung Patrick, and aroused him to write the "Declaration" that defended his ministry.

What was the "beef" of the British Church leaders? They

seemed to have defined two roles (only) for a bishop: administrator and chaplain. Therefore, a bishop's primary (perhaps only) expectations were to administer the existing churches and care for faithful Christians. (A local priest's job description was similar, stressing pastoral care of the local flock.) So the British leaders were offended and angered that Patrick was spending priority time with "pagans," "sinners," and "barbarians."

This perspective had surfaced four centuries earlier. Jesus had been savagely criticized by the Pharisees for practicing the same kind of fraternizing priorities that Patrick now practiced. Furthermore, this perspective is widespread today. Pastors and churches, today, who regard outreach to lost people as the church's main business, and especially those who are perceived to prefer the company of lost people to the company of church people, are suspect, marginalized, and "shot at" by establishment Christians and church leaders. No major denomination in the United States regards apostolic ministry to pre-Christian outsiders as its "priority" or even as "normal" ministry.

THINK   *"Wouldn't you leave the ninety-nine in the wilderness and go after the lost one until you found it?"*

- Who are the presumed "unreachables" in your geographical area? Why is this the stereotype?
- What are most of the churches, or the "ninety-nine," in your area doing in regard to these "barbarians"? Are the ones who are doing something trying to reach them or "civilize" them?
- Do you feel drawn to people who are lost? Why or why not?
- If you chose to "leave the ninety-nine . . . and go after the lost," do you think you would have any support? If so, who or where would that come from? What makes you think this?

THINK (continued)

PRAY

Look back at the "Think" sections. Ruminate on your responses. Let them distill into a prayer, and then write that prayer below.

Friend of sinners . . .

The issue of prayer is not prayer; the issue of prayer is God.

ABRAHAM HESCHEL

LIVE

"Wouldn't you leave the ninety-nine in the wilderness and go after the lost one until you found it?"

The challenge now is to take this question further along—to live out this question. Think of one thing, *just one*, that you can personally do to wrestle with the question, inhabit the character of it, and live it in everyday life. In the following space, jot down your thoughts on this "one thing." Read the quotes that follow for additional inspiration. During the coming week, pray about this "one thing," talk with a close friend about it, and learn to live the question.

One thing . . .

Go to the people.
Live among them.
Learn from them.
Love them.
Start with what they know.
Build on what they have.

Chinese poem

> Live the questions now. Perhaps you will then gradually, without noticing it, live along some distant day into the answer.
> RAINER MARIA RILKE, *LETTERS TO A YOUNG POET*

LESSON 9

"But how much of that kind of persistent faith will the Son of Man find on the earth when he returns?" (Luke 18:8)

Before You Begin

Take some time to reflect and prepare your heart and mind for this study. Read the following Scripture passage. Soak up God's Word. There's no hurry. Then, when you're ready, turn the page and begin.

James 5:16-18

Make this your common practice: Confess your sins to each other and pray for each other so that you can live together whole and healed. The prayer of a person living right with God is something powerful to be reckoned with. Elijah, for instance, human just like us, prayed hard that it wouldn't rain, and it didn't—not a drop for three and a half years. Then he prayed that it would rain, and it did. The showers came and everything started growing again.

READ

Luke 18:1-8

Jesus told them a story showing that it was necessary for them to pray consistently and never quit. He said, "There was once a judge in some city who never gave God a thought and cared nothing for people. A widow in that city kept after him: 'My rights are being violated. Protect me!'

"He never gave her the time of day. But after this went on and on he said to himself, 'I care nothing what God thinks, even less what people think. But because this widow won't quit badgering me, I'd better do something and see that she gets justice—otherwise I'm going to end up beaten black and blue by her pounding.'"

Then the Master said, "Do you hear what that judge, corrupt as he is, is saying? So what makes you think God won't step in and work justice for his chosen people, who continue to cry out for help? Won't he stick up for them? I assure you, he will. He will not drag his feet. **But how much of that kind of persistent faith will the Son of Man find on the earth when he returns?**"

THINK   *"But how much of that kind of persistent faith will the Son of Man find on the earth when he returns?"*

- What is your immediate response to this question?
- Why do you think you responded in this way?
- Why do you think Jesus told this story? Why do you think he chose to use a widow in the story?
- How do you deal with people who won't quit badgering you?
- Do you badger God when you pray?

THINK (continued)

READ

From *The Wizard's Tide*, by Frederick Buechner[1]

After a while, she asked Teddy what he had been doing lately. She didn't ask it just to be polite the way grown-ups often do but because when she took a fancy to people, she liked listening to them almost as much as she liked talking. So Teddy told her. He told her how his father had been trying to teach him the proper way to ride waves, and he told her how he had been rolled by a couple of them and what it had felt like while it was going on.

"I can hardly think of anything under the sun I would less want to do myself even if I could swim, which I can't, just like your dear mother," Dan said. "I would pay cash money to get out of it."

"It's scary all right," Teddy said. "But Daddy says if you don't fight the waves they'll always bring you back to shore because that's where they're going too."

"Well, I suppose that's true," Dan said. "But it would be just like me to get caught in a sea puss instead, I'm afraid."

Teddy had rather big eyes, and sometimes they were apt to get even bigger.

"What's that?" he said.

"Why it's the undertow, my poor ignorant boy," she said. "The waves bring you in all right if you know what you're doing, but there's always a sea puss somewhere just licking its chops for a chance to drag some respectable matron who doesn't know how to swim the other way."

"There are a lot more waves than there are sea pusses though," Teddy said, "and they're much stronger."

"Of course they are," she said. "And what's more, the sea pusses always give up after a while but the waves never do."

Dan had let the ash on her cigarette grow so long that when she moved her hand, it fell off onto the arm of her green rocker.

"It's also a rule of life that no matter how far the low tide goes out," she said, "the high tide always comes in again as high as ever. I suppose that's a handy thing to remember when you're feeling a little low yourself."

"Do you feel low ever, Dan?" Teddy asked.

"Sometimes I feel like going out in the garden and chewing worms," she said.

"I wish bad things didn't happen," Teddy said.

"It would be nice, there's no question about that," Dan said. "But the way things are, I guess all you can do is wait for them to unhappen. In the long run they usually seem to."

"I guess so," Teddy said.

"And in the meantime, make yourself scarce if you see a sea puss heading in your direction," she said. "And try to catch the tide at the flow."

"The one that brings you in," Teddy said.

"The very one," Dan said.

THINK
"But how much of that kind of persistent faith will the Son of Man find on the earth when he returns?"

- Just so you know, Teddy's father in this story committed suicide. When he says, "I wish bad things didn't happen," that's what he's referring to.
- What bad or scary things are going on in your life right now? Are any of your rights being violated? Do you feel unprotected?
- How strong are the "sea pusses" (the "undertow"), and what effect are they having on your prayer life?
- Read this again: "And what's more, the sea pusses always give up after a while but the waves never do." Compare it to what Jesus said: "So what makes you think God won't step in and work justice for his chosen people, who continue to cry out for help? Won't he stick up for them? I assure you, he will."
- Bad things happen. What would it take for you to persist in crying out and to "wait for them to unhappen"?

- Do you find it easy or difficult to trust that the waves—that God—will "always bring you back to shore"? Why?

READ

From *A Long Obedience in the Same Direction*, by Eugene H. Peterson[2]

It is not difficult in such a world to get a person interested in the message of the gospel; it is terribly difficult to sustain the interest. Millions of people in our culture make decisions for Christ, but there is a dreadful attrition rate. Many claim to have been born again, but the evidence for mature Christian discipleship is slim. In our kind of culture anything, even news about God, can be sold if it is packaged freshly; but when it loses its novelty, it goes on the garbage heap. There is a great market for religious experience in our world; there is little enthusiasm for the patient acquisition of virtue, little inclination to sign up for a long apprenticeship in what earlier generations of Christians called holiness.

Religion in our time has been captured by the tourist mindset. Religion is understood as a visit to an attractive site to be made when we have adequate leisure. For some it is a weekly jaunt to church. For others, occasional visits to special services. Some, with a bent for religious entertainment and sacred diversion, plan their lives around special events like retreats, rallies, and conferences. We go to see a new personality, to hear a new truth, to get a new experience and so, somehow, expand our otherwise humdrum lives. The religious life is defined as the latest and the newest: Zen, faith-healing, human potential, parapsychology, successful living, choreography in the chancel, Armageddon. We'll try anything—until something else comes along.

I don't know what it has been like for pastors in other cultures and previous centuries, but I am quite sure that for a pastor in Western culture in the latter part of the twentieth century the aspect of *world* that makes the work of leading Christians in the way of faith most difficult is what Gore Vidal has analyzed as "today's passion for the immediate and the casual." Everyone is in a hurry. The persons whom I lead in worship, among whom I counsel, visit, pray, preach, and teach, want short cuts. They want me to help them fill out the form that will get them instant credit (in eternity). They are impatient for results. They have adopted the lifestyle of a tourist and only want the high points. But a pastor is not a tour guide. I have no interest in telling apocryphal religious stories at and around dubiously identified sacred sites. The Christian life cannot mature under such conditions and in such ways.

Friedrich Nietzsche, who saw this area of spiritual truth, at least, with great clarity wrote, "The essential thing 'in heaven and earth' is . . . that there should be long obedience in the same direction; there thereby results, and has always resulted in the long run, something which has made life worth living."[3] It is this "long obedience in the same direction" which the mood of the world does so much to discourage.

THINK   "But how much of that kind of persistent faith will the Son of Man find on the earth when he returns?"

- Do you agree with Peterson? Why or why not?
- "Everyone . . . want[s] short cuts." What short cuts are you seeking right now in your Christian life? In your prayer life specifically? Where are you impatient for results?
- Think about some ways in which the mood of the world discourages "long obedience in the same direction." Now substitute the word *persistence* for *obedience* and list as many ways as you can.
- Don't miss Nietzsche's (and Peterson's) clarity: "Long obedience in the same direction . . . has always resulted in . . . something which has made life worth living."

THINK (continued)

READ

From *Deep Memory, Exuberant Hope*, by Walter Brueggemann[4]

1. Elie Wiesel has spent his life in determination that the barbaric reality of the Jewish holocaust shall not be forgotten. He has observed that the truth of the Holocaust is deeply disputed and there are those who insist it never happened. More than that, he has observed that the truth of the Holocaust depends completely upon the witnesses, people who are not sophisticated but who are credible through the character of their testimony, through their capacity to tell credibly how it was with them.

2. A great deal of attention has been given to the practice of "stories of woundedness" among those who are ill and who require medical attention. "Scientific medicine," rather like "consensus theological truth," has had no need of stories, because it operated out of the "truth of medicine" that was established "from above," as was theological truth. Without denying the important claims of scientific medicine, more recent observers have noticed that suffering people need to tell the story of suffering so as to engage others in a relatedness of suffering whereby healing may happen as a relational phenomenon. Indeed, in his book *The Wounded Storyteller*, Arthur Frank has offered a chapter entitled "testimony," giving evidence of the ways a sufferer must construe reality "from below," that is, out of pain.

3. The other day I was in a bank teller line at noon, observing to the woman next to me in line how most bank tellers took long lunch breaks just when I wanted one to be available. That comment triggered in the woman behind me, whom I did not know, the opportunity for her to tell me her story of being cheated by a fast-food place out of fifty dollars of low-pay wages and to report that she never got a lunch break. She then told me that she planned to bring a suit against the company for having cheated her. She said, "I will probably lose, but I will have been heard." She told me that message three times in four minutes. She was giving "testimony," and she would give

more of it in court, stating her bid for truth. It was, moreover, urgent that she be heard, even if the fast-food company would be dominant in court, as she herself anticipated. She will have been heard with her version of truth!

Notice in all three cases, testimony comes as a truth "from below" in the face of a "stronger truth" that is hegemonic:

Jewish *survivors* amid scientific analysis of what
     happened
sufferers amid medical science
the *"cheated woman"* in the face of a powerful fast-food
     chain

Each of these witnesses makes a bid for a version of the truth.

Such testimony is characteristically:

Fragile. It depends upon the nerve of the teller.
Local. It makes no sweeping, universal claim but appeals
     to what is concretely known.
Persuasive. The rhetorical casting aims at winning the
     jury.
Contested. It dares utterance in the presence of other
     claims that may be more powerful and more
     credible.
Fragmented. It is only a bit of a narrative that brings with
     it a whole theory of reality that is implied but left
     unexpressed.

Such claims for truth are not loud, arrogant, or sweeping. They are modest but insistent and sometimes compelling.

THINK   "But how much of that kind of persistent faith will the Son of Man find on the earth when he returns?"

- Consider this: A person of persistent faith is one who bears witness, or gives testimony, out of his or her pain.
- Brueggemann gives three examples of testimony in the face of stronger, or hegemonic, truth. Think about your prayer life. When have you been outnumbered by stronger or hegemonic voices but have continued to pray or give testimony to God's truth?
- Brueggemann's concluding characteristics are incredible ammo for the believer who aspires to persistent faith when the Son of Man returns. In light of these, consider the following questions: Have you lost your prayer nerve? Are your prayers composed of the real stuff or theological verbiage? Do you want more than to simply "be heard"?

PRAY

Look back at the "Think" sections. Ruminate on your responses. Let them distill into a prayer, and then write that prayer below.

Son of Man . . .

The issue of prayer is not prayer; the issue of prayer is God.

ABRAHAM HESCHEL

LIVE

"But how much of that kind of persistent faith will the Son of Man find on the earth when he returns?"

The challenge now is to take this question further along—to live out this question. Think of one thing, *just one*, that you can personally do to wrestle with the question, inhabit the character of it, and live it in everyday life. In the following space, jot down your thoughts on this "one thing." Read the quotes that follow for additional inspiration. During the coming week, pray about this "one thing," talk with a close friend about it, and learn to live the question.

One thing...

The purpose of such incessant testimony is to nurture and sustain one another in odd vision, because without such nurture and sustenance, it is for sure that members of the community will fall out of this truth into other more attractive, more palatable, less costly truth.

Walter Brueggemann

There is a religious word for what I have been describing: *supplication*. Supplication means to ask with earnestness, with intensity, with perseverance. It is a declaration that we are deadly serious about this prayer business.

Richard Foster

Live the questions now. Perhaps you will then gradually, without noticing it, live along some distant day into the answer.

RAINER MARIA RILKE, *LETTERS TO A YOUNG POET*

LESSON 10

"What do *you* want?" (Luke 22:42)

Before You Begin

Take some time to reflect and prepare your heart and mind for this study. Read the following Scripture passage. Soak up God's Word. There's no hurry. Then, when you're ready, turn the page and begin.

Micah 6:8

> But he's already made it plain how to live, what to do,
>> what God is looking for in men and women.
> It's quite simple: Do what is fair and just to your neighbor,
>> be compassionate and loyal in your love,
> And don't take yourself too seriously—
>> take God seriously.

READ

Luke 22:33-46

Peter said, "Master, I'm ready for anything with you. I'd go to jail for you. I'd *die* for you!"

Jesus said, "I'm sorry to have to tell you this, Peter, but before the rooster crows you will have three times denied that you know me."

Then Jesus said, "When I sent you out and told you to travel light, to take only the bare necessities, did you get along all right?"

"Certainly," they said, "we got along just fine."

He said, "This is different. Get ready for trouble. Look to what you'll need; there are difficult times ahead. Pawn your coat and get a sword. What was written in Scripture, 'He was lumped in with the criminals,' gets its final meaning in me. Everything written about me is now coming to a conclusion."

They said, "Look, Master, two swords!"

But he said, "Enough of that; no more sword talk!"

Leaving there, he went, as he so often did, to Mount Olives. The disciples followed him. When they arrived at the place, he said, "Pray that you don't give in to temptation."

He pulled away from them about a stone's throw, knelt down, and prayed, "Father, remove this cup from me. But please, not what I want. **What do *you* want?**" At once an angel from heaven was at his side, strengthening him. He prayed on all the harder. Sweat, wrung from him like drops of blood, poured off his face.

He got up from prayer, went back to the disciples and found them asleep, drugged by grief. He said, "What business do you have sleeping? Get up. Pray so you won't give in to temptation."

THINK   "What do *you* want?"

- What is your immediate response to this question?
- Why do you think you responded in this way?
- What word would you use to describe the tone of this passage? Why?
- Why do you think Jesus pulled away from the disciples to pray?
- Let's take Peter's statement and compare it to Jesus' prayer: "Master, I'm ready for anything with you. I'd go to jail for you. I'd *die* for you!" "Father, remove this cup from me. But please, not what I want. What do *you* want?" Take some time to do a comparison/contrast. Write down everything you think of.
- Jesus knew what God's will was. But do you think we ever really know? Why or why not?

READ

From *A Traveler Toward the Dawn*, by William J. O'Malley, S.J.[1]

July 12, Friday morning. I'm alone in the parish *casa* before the fireplace copying into my journal significant quotes from the Medellin documents. This landmark 1968 meeting of the South American bishops translated Vatican II spirit into the Latin American experience. This one sentence seems to me to sum up best what I've been experiencing in Zunil for the last two weeks: "Latin America lives under the tragic sign of underdevelopment, a compounding of hunger and misery, illness of a massive nature and widespread infant mortality, of illiteracy and marginality, or profound inequality of income. . . ."

Suddenly the door bell clangs. Diego, age twenty-eight, father of three, stands there with a big smile on his face. "Padre Juan, will you come over to the church this afternoon for a blessing?" In my halting Spanish, I assure him I will and ask him what the blessing is all about. "Padre," he says with the same smile, "it is for my little *niña* who died last night." "Oh, no, Diego, not your lovely little eleven-year-old daughter? This is terrible." Diego's eyes mist over, "Padre, it is God's will. We must not be angry with God; now my family has a little angel in heaven."

I go back to the rectory with fists clenched. I feel like punching out the first window I see. If there is one thing God does not will, I'm sure, it is the needless death of these lovely malnourished children, haunted by the spectre of dysentery and virus. How needless this all is; yet day by day the relentless statistic: two of every three kids of this town die early. I'm sick of burying beautiful little children in stark wooden boxes. Yet I'm staggered somehow at the simplicity of Diego's faith.

So, that afternoon in the silent church, I say the words of consolation over the little crate box, grieving in my heart with Diego. "Eternal rest grant unto this little one; Lord, let your perpetual light shine upon her; I am the resurrection and the life. The one who believes in me will live even if she dies; may the angels lead you home to paradise; may the martyrs come out to welcome you."

After the blessing Diego comes up to me all smiles and thanks me and gives me a *quetzal* bill which I don't at all want to accept and then invites me outside to a surprising sight. A procession was formed into one long line, complete with a six piece oompah band playing joyous music. The whole troupe takes off, band first tooting away, then the crude wooden box, then Diego and his wife and relatives and mourners. A pitiful, strangely joyous service for the little *niña* who is now "an angel in heaven."

I go back to the rectory torn inside, grieving for Diego and wondering at the staggering faith of the Mayan yet angry at a system that kills as surely as a machine-gun burst.

THINK   *"What do you want?"*

- Re-read Diego's statement: "Padre, it is God's will." How do you feel about that?
- Re-read Eagan's words: "If there is one thing God does not will, I'm sure, it is the needless death of these lovely malnourished children." How do you feel about his thoughts?
- How do you understand God's will? This is a question that has been wrestled with throughout the ages. Just answer in terms of your life. What does God's will mean to you?
- How do you go about discovering it?

READ

From *Walking on Water*, by Madeleine L'Engle[2]

I doubt if there's any such thing as total objectivity. We listen out of our own skins, our own ears, see through our own eyes with their various myopias and astigmatisms. A history of either the English or American Civil War will show a totally different war when told from the point of view of one side or the other. The villains of one book will be the protagonists of the other. The historian trying to show both points of view fairly is still caught within his own subjective interpretations. We come more closely to a clear view in the novels of Dostoyevsky, Robertson Davies, the plays of Shakespeare.

In an interview in a well-known Christian magazine, I explained earnestly that we are limited by our points of view; "I have a point of view," I told the interviewer, "You have a point of view. But God has *view*." When the article appeared, some over-diligent copy editor had changed it to, "I have a point of view. You have a point of view. God has a point of view."

I wrote back in a white heat. "This is a theological error. Please correct it. The *point is* . . ."

In our daily living the actions we choose, from within our own skins, as the best possible under the circumstances, may well turn out to have been the wrong ones. Something we regret at the time as abysmally stupid may well end up being the one thing needed under the circumstances. We are trapped in unknowing. . . .

It is a criterion of love. In moments of decision, we are to try to make what seems to be the most loving, the most creative decision. We are not to play safe, to draw back out of fear. Love may well lead us into danger. It may lead us to die for our friend. In a day when we are taught to look for easy solutions, it is not always easy to hold on to that most difficult one of all, love.

During a summer session at Wheaton, one of the students asked, "Do you think there are any absolutes?"

I thought for a second and then said, off the top of my head, "Yes, I think the ten commandments are absolutes." Later, as I set them against the great works of literature, they seemed to hold fast. When we break one of the commandments, we are . . . being destructive, rather than creative. We are taking things into our own hands and playing God. Playing God, hubris, presumption, the tragic flow of all the great Greek heroes. But having broken the first commandment, it is almost inevitable that the breaking of others will follow. Oedipus dishonors both his parents. Anna Karenina commits adultery. Macbeth is covetous. Dorian Gray makes a graven image of himself. Iago bears false witness against his neighbour. And so it goes. Whenever the first commandment is broken, more breakage follows. We are, as a consequence, unable to love ourselves, and so we are not able to love our neighbour.

We take things into our own hands. We listen to promises of security, promises that can only be false. We forget those absolutes against which we can set our behaviour, make our decisions. And we lose heart, and are no longer able to pluck, out of the nettle, danger, the flower of courage.

And we draw back.

At school in Charleston I was running, tripped, and fell through a window. I picked myself up in a shower of glass, and did not have a scratch on me because I did not have time to draw back. If I had, I would have been cut, and badly.

THINK   "What do *you* want?"

- "I doubt if there's any such thing as total objectivity." Do you agree with this statement? Why or why not?
- When you find yourself "trapped in un-knowing," do you "draw back out of fear" and play it safe? What causes that reaction?
- What is your reaction to L'Engle's statement that "love may well lead us . . . to die for our friend"? Has God's will led you in that direction before?

- Think about this: L'Engle states that drawing back results in a lack of faith and a loss of heart. Could a loss of heart possibly be what God wants?

READ

From *Holy the Firm*, by Annie Dillard[3]

Today is Friday, November 20. Julie Norwich is in the hospital, burned; we can get no word of her condition. People released from burn wards, I read once, have a very high suicide rate. They had not realized, before they were burned, that life could include such suffering, not that they personally could be permitted such pain. No drugs ease the pain of third-degree burns, because burns destroy skin: the drugs simply leak into the sheets. His disciples asked Christ about a roadside beggar who had been blind from birth, "Who did sin, this man or his parents, that he was born blind?" And Christ, who spat on the ground, made a mud of his spittle and clay, plastered the mud over the man's eyes, and gave him sight, answered, "Neither hath this man sinned, nor his parents: but that the works of God should be made manifest in him." Really? If we take this answer to refer to the affliction itself—and not the subsequent cure—as "God's works made manifest," then we have, along with "Not as the world gives do I give unto you," two meager, baffling, and infuriating answers to one of the few questions worth asking, to wit, What in the Sam Hill is going on here?

The works of God made manifest? Do we really need more victims to remind us that we're all victims? Is this some sort of parade for which a conquering army shines up its terrible guns and rolls them up and down the streets for the people to see? Do we need blind men stumbling about, and little flamefaced children, to remind us what God can—and will—do?

I am drinking boiled coffee and watching the bay from the window. Almost all of the people who reef net have hauled their gears for the winter; the salmon runs are over, days are short. Still, boats come and go on the water—tankers, tugs and barges, rowboats and sails. There are killer whales if you're lucky, rafts of harlequin ducks if you're lucky, and every day the scoter and the solitary grebes. How many tons of sky can I see from the window? It is morning: morning! and the water clobbered with light. Yes, in fact, we do. We do need reminding, not of what God can do, but of what he cannot do, or will not, which is to catch time in its free fall and stick a nickel's worth of sense into our days. And we need reminding of what time can do, must only do; churn out enormity at random and beat it, with God's blessing, into our heads: that we are created, *created*, sojourners in a land we did not make, a land with no meaning of itself and no meaning we can make for it alone. Who are we to demand explanations of God? (And what monsters of perfection should we be if we did not?) We forget ourselves, picnicking; we forget where we are. There is no such thing as a freak accident. "God is at home," says Meister Eckhart, "We are in the far country."

We are most deeply asleep at the switch when we fancy we control any switches at all. We sleep to time's hurdy-gurdy; we wake, if we ever wake, to the silence of God. And then, when we wake to the deep shores of light uncreated, then when the dazzling dark breaks over the far slopes of time, then it's time to toss things, like our reason, and our will; then it's time to break our necks for home.

THINK   *"What do you want?"*

- A note of background: Julie Norwich was a neighbor of Dillard's who was badly burned in an airplane crash.
- What words or phrases from Dillard's essay move you? Why?
- What can you take away from her words concerning what God wants, or what God wills?
- Dillard says, "There is no such thing as a freak accident." What do you think? Why?
- Dillard has a Job-like moment: "We are created, *created*, sojourners in a land we did not make, a land with no meaning of itself and no meaning we can make for it alone. Who are we to demand explanations of God?" Maybe, just maybe, our best

hope is to say, "Not what I want. What do *you* want?"—to not draw back in fear but to run at breakneck speed for home, into the arms of our Abba. Rest in these thoughts for a while.

PRAY

Look back at the "Think" sections. Ruminate on your responses. Let them distill into a prayer, and then write that prayer below.

Thy will be done on earth as in heaven . . .

The issue of prayer is not prayer; the issue of prayer is God.

ABRAHAM HESCHEL

LIVE   "What do *you* want?"

The challenge now is to take this question further along—to live out this question. Think of one thing, *just one*, that you can personally do to wrestle with the question, inhabit the character of it, and live it in everyday life. In the following space, jot down your thoughts on this "one thing." Read the quotes that follow for additional inspiration. During the coming week, pray about this "one thing," talk with a close friend about it, and learn to live the question.

One thing . . .

But all shall be well and all shall be well and all manner of thing shall be well.

Lady Julian of Norwich

I have a point of view. You have a point of view. But God has *view*.

Madeleine L'Engle

Live the questions now. Perhaps you will then gradually, without noticing it, live along some distant day into the answer.

Rainer Maria Rilke, *Letters to a Young Poet*

NOTES

LESSON 1

1. Wendell Berry, *In the Presence of Fear: Three Essays for a Changed World* (Great Barrington, MA: The Orion Society, 2001), 6–9.
2. Barry Lopez, *Resistance* (New York: Knopf, 2004), 8–10.
3. Frederick Buechner, *The Clown in the Belfry: Writings on Faith and Fiction* (New York: HarperCollins, 1992), 147–148.

LESSON 2

1. Brian D. McLaren, *A New Kind of Christian: A Tale of Two Friends on a Spiritual Journey* (New York: Wiley, 2001), 12–13.
2. Mark Buchanan, *Your God Is Too Safe* (Sisters, OR: Multnomah, 2001), 32–33.
3. C. S. Lewis, *The Lion, the Witch and the Wardrobe*, first Collier Books ed. (1950; repr., New York: Macmillan, 1970), 75–76.

LESSON 3

1. Mike Yaconelli, *Messy Spirituality: God's Annoying Love for Imperfect People* (Grand Rapids, MI: Zondervan, 2002), 33–34.
2. Robert Farrar Capon, *Between Noon and Three: Romance, Law, and the Outrage of Grace* (Grand Rapids, MI: Eerdmans, 1997), 143–145.
3. Richard Rohr and Joseph Martos, *The Wild Man's Journey: Reflections on Male Spirituality* (Cincinnati, OH: St. Anthony Messenger Press, 1992), 41.

LESSON 4

1. Harper Lee, *To Kill a Mockingbird* (Philadelphia: J. B. Lippincott Co., 1960), 292–293.
2. James Hillman, *Insearch: Psychology and Religion* (Woodstock, CT: Spring Publications Inc., 1994), 75–77.
3. Thomas Moore, *Care of the Soul: A Guide for Cultivating Depth and Sacredness in Everyday Life* (New York: HarperCollins, 1992), 14.

LESSON 5

1. Eugene H. Peterson, *Working the Angles: The Shape of Pastoral Integrity* (Grand Rapids, MI: Eerdmans, 1987), 45–50.
2. Frederick Buechner, *Listening to Your Life: Daily Meditations with Frederick Buechner*, comp. George Connor (New York: HarperSanFranscisco, 1992), 78–79.

LESSON 6

1. Ray Bradbury, *Fahrenheit 451* (New York: Ballantine Books, 1953), 87–89.
2. James Kavanaugh, "There Are Men Too Gentle to Live Among Wolves" in *There Are Men Too Gentle to Live Among Wolves* (Highland Park, IL: Steven J. Nash Publishing, 1970).

LESSON 7

1. Gerald G. May, MD, *The Awakened Heart: Opening Yourself to the Love You Need* (New York: HarperCollins, 1991), 222–223.
2. C. S. Lewis, *The Four Loves: The Much Beloved Exploration of the Nature of Love* (Orlando, FL: Harcourt, 1960), 123–124.
3. David James Duncan, *The River Why* (San Francisco: Sierra Club Books, 1983), 238–239, 243–245.

LESSON 8

1. John Steinbeck, *Of Mice and Men* (Shelton, CT: Viking Penguin Books USA Inc., 1937), 27–30.
2. Lesslie Newbigin, *The Gospel in a Pluralist Society* (Grand Rapids, MI: Eerdmans, 1989), 82–83.

3. George G. Hunter III, *The Celtic Way of Evangelism: How Christianity Can Reach the West . . . Again* (Nashville: Abingdon, 2000), 18–19, 23–24.

4. Thomas Cahill, *How the Irish Saved Civilization* (New York: Doubleday, 1995), 82.

LESSON 9

1. Frederick Buechner, *The Wizard's Tide: A Story* (New York: HarperCollins, 1990), 63–64.

2. Eugene H. Peterson, *A Long Obedience in the Same Direction: Discipleship in an Instant Society* (Downers Grove, IL: InterVarsity, 1980), 12–13.

3. Friedrich Nietzsche, *Beyond Good and Evil*, trans. Helen Zimmern (London, 1907), section 188, 106–109.

4. Walter Brueggemann, *Deep Memory, Exuberant Hope: Contested Truth in a Post-Christian World* (Minneapolis: Augsburg, 2000), 20–21.

LESSON 10

1. William J. O'Malley, S.J., *A Traveler Toward the Dawn: The Spiritual Journal of John Eagan, S.J.* (Chicago: Loyola University Press, 1990), 45–47.

2. Madeleine L'Engle, *Walking on Water: Reflections on Faith and Art* (Wheaton, IL: Shaw, 1980), 151–154.

3. Annie Dillard, *Holy the Firm* (New York: Harper & Row, 1977), 59–62.

GROW STRONGER IN YOUR FAITH BY WRESTLING WITH LIFE'S BIGGEST QUESTIONS.

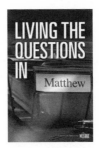

Living the Questions
in Matthew
1-57683-833-1

Living the Questions
in Mark
1-57683-860-9

Living the Questions
in John
1-57683-834-X

Jesus asked more questions than he ever answered outright. Now readers and study groups can wrestle with some of these issues with these intriguing new studies of the Gospels based on *The Message*— the eye-opening translation by Eugene Peterson. Through these compelling studies, readers can embrace life's questions and build a stronger faith.

Visit your local Christian bookstore,
call NavPress at 1-800-366-7788, or log on to www.navpress.com
to purchase.

To locate a Christian bookstore near you, call 1-800-991-7747.

NAVPRESS
BRINGING TRUTH TO LIFE
www.navpress.com